SHORT FILMS
101

SHORT FILMS
101

*How to Make a Short Film
and Launch
Your Filmmaking Career*

FREDERICK LEVY

A PERIGEE BOOK

A Perigee Book
Published by The Berkley Publishing Group
A division of Penguin Group (USA) Inc.
375 Hudson Street
New York, New York 10014

Perigee trade paperback edition: May 2004

Library of Congress Cataloging-in-Publication Data

Levy, Frederick.
    Short films 101: how to make a short film for under 50K—and launch
your screenwriting career / by Frederick Levy.
        p. cm.
    ISBN 0-399-52949-7
    1. Motion pictures—Production and direction. 2. Short films.
I. Title: Short films one hundred one. II. Title.

PN1995.9.P7L436 2004
791.43'02'3—dc22   2003070654

Printed in the United States of America

10   9   8   7   6   5   4   3   2   1

For my parents, Lois and Barry Levy. I love you.

And for anyone with a camera and a dream.

Contents

Contents

Acknowledgments

I'D LIKE TO THANK the following people for helping make this book possible: my agent, Andrée Abecassis; my editor, Michelle Howry; and my friend and mentor, James Robert Parish. Thank you for helping me see this project through to fruition.

Those experts who shared their valuable experience and stories: Gary Bryman, Luke Greenfield, Bryan Gordon, Eric Haase, Steve Hein, Gene Klein, Eric Kripke, Peter Lord, Jana Sue Memel, Mike Mitchell, Joe Nussbaum, Susan Peterson, Eduardo Rodriguez, Mika Salmi, Trevor Sands, and Adam Stein.

Those who helped me coordinate different aspects of my research: Kathleen Barber, Alison Cook, Alex Heineman, Ryan Lichterman, Bill Narducci, Dan Rabinow, Dave Scotti, Brad Simon, Sarah Jane Sluke, Craig Mizrahi, and Kevin Wendle.

The entire team at Management 101; all our talented clients; my publicist, Kirsten Andresen; my web guru and friend, Andrew Putschoegl; and my hardworking assistants: Jonathan Angus, David Cox, Melissa Kawasoe, Jennie Mosely, and Rashad Raisani.

And last, but not least, my family and friends. Thanks for your love and support, for understanding why I lock myself away for six months while I write, and for still being there when I reemerge.

AS A FILM EXECUTIVE, I have been amazed over the last few years at how many filmmakers have gotten the opportunity to direct feature films based on the strength of their low-budget short. When Dimension Films announced in 2002 that they were giving Eduardo Rodriguez a three-picture deal because they loved his student film, my curiosity was more than piqued. I was determined to discover what was so special about these particular films and filmmakers that warranted them getting these amazing opportunities in the feature arena.

The first thing I did was watch a whole lot of short films. Shorts are easier to view today than ever before. Between the Internet, film festivals, and various cable television channels (IFC, Sundance, HBO, etc.), I was never at a loss for material to analyze. I found that there was a difference in the quality of the films that were randomly posted to the Internet and those that got cable distribution. After screening many of the films that be-got studio deals, I began to understand what made a short film capable of launching a filmmaking career.

I started to read books on film production, and although many were proficient in instructing how to technically make a movie, none of them really delved into the real explanation of how to use that film to grab Hollywood's attention. I was also amazed at how many books encouraged novices to make a low-budget feature rather than start with a much more practical and even more effective short. I saw a need for a book from an industry insider's perspective that focused on the end goal: making a short film to help you land the deal.

This is *not* a book on the techniques of filmmaking. Many tips on making movies are revealed in the pages of this text, but this is not a practical how-to guide for making films. Instead, this is a book specific to the short form for people who are already familiar with the basic filmmaking principals.

This book is for anyone who is serious about building a career in filmmaking. The way I see it, you have two choices: You can continue to create moving images in a vacuum and hope you stumble onto something that strikes a chord with Hollywood executives, or you can carefully plan to make a short with the main intention of using the finished piece as a "calling card" to a professional opportunity.

I shall lend much of my own personal experience to the text. I have been involved with many major motion pictures, including *Titanic, Reindeer Games,* and *Frailty.* In my current position at Management 101, I am responsible for guiding the careers of both established and up-and-coming filmmakers. As the prolific author of several film industry books, I have my finger on the pulse of what readers want to know about establishing filmmaking careers.

This book also contains the advice of a variety of Hollywood insiders who got their starts in short films, from *The Animal* director Luke Greenfield to *Chicken Run* helmer Peter Lord. They did not all succeed on their first try, but they each completed a short that helped launch their professional careers. After reading this book, I hope you will gain the insight to apply these methods to your own short films. If you do, I believe you will increase your chances of finding success in the professional arena.

Many of the short films discussed in the text can be found online. Some of them are available for purchase on VHS and DVD. Making an attempt to view the shorts we discuss will certainly be helpful, but it is not imperative that you be familiar with them to understand the book. If you come across any jargon you are unfamiliar with, you will find a glossary at the end of the book. Finally, any and all updates to this book can be found on our website at www.fredericklevy.com, which also serves as an addendum to this book.

My hope is that the insight you gain from reading this book will help you forge a successful filmmaking career. Enjoy the read.

Getting Started:
Why Make a Short Film?

"Today everybody has a video camera, which makes for a lot of armchair Hollywood quarterbacks who would like to have a creative outlet to put content together."

—Adam Stein, executive vice president, IFilm

EPISODE I

A short time ago, in a galaxy not too far away (Los Angeles, to be exact), an aspiring filmmaker named Joe Nussbaum was contemplating his future. Having gone to film school to become a director, he was now making a living writing and producing trailers—for other directors' movies. But boys can dream, as Joe often did about his own big screen career.

For someone only a few years out of film school, Joe was doing relatively well. An internship with Beacon Pictures the summer before he graduated led to his first industry job there as an assistant to a creative executive. Though he learned a lot that would help him later in his career, he did not feel his administrative position was helping keep his creative juices fresh.

While working in development, Joe witnessed a new phenomenon that was creating a great deal of buzz around town. Short films were landing on the desks of Hollywood executives, and the best ones were being passed around development circles. An early favorite that garnered a great deal of publicity was *Troops,* a hilarious spoof of the TV show *Cops* featuring *Star Wars* Storm Troopers patrolling the planet of Tatooine. Amazed with the response these films were receiving from the industry and the attention being paid to the filmmakers, Nussbaum began to formulate a plan to capitalize on this new trend.

Nussbaum wasn't the only person whose brain was churning. Advancements in technology provided broadband connections to a greater number of people. The Internet was gradually replacing television as the leading source of home entertainment. And although patience wore thin waiting for lengthy video files to download, the web seemed like the perfect distribution outlet for short films.

Every week another website featuring short form original content seemed to appear. Film parodies like *Saving Ryan's Privates* and *Swing Blade,* a spoof of the movies *Swingers* and *Sling Blade,* found homes online where the masses could watch them. Companies like AtomFilms and IFilm were creating business plans to make Internet distribution of short films profitable.

But the most exciting development was that many of the movies appearing online were coming from outside of Hollywood. Film fans around the globe had a brand-new entrée to Tinsel Town. They could make a film in their own backyard, upload it to the web, and get discovered. These short films really were getting noticed, and they were generating some genuine Hollywood success stories.

- Mike Mitchell posted his short film *Herd* online, attracting the attention of Columbia Pictures and landing him a job directing *Deuce Bigalow: Male Gigolo.*

- Between self-distribution on tape and a successful run on the Internet, the short film *George Lucas in Love* helped get Joe Nussbaum attached to direct several studio features.

- Luke Greenfield's short film, *The Right Hook,* was the reason he got to direct *The Animal* starring Rob Schneider.

This is more than just a book about how to make a short film. Anyone with a camera and an idea can make a short. This book is about making the *right* short and effectively using it to launch your professional career in Hollywood.

This might be easier said than done. I shall follow the journeys of several filmmakers who approached Hollywood with the strategy outlined in the pages of this book. I will examine what they did right, what they did wrong, and how you can learn from their experiences to formulate your own filmmaking plan.

Remember, the entertainment business is extremely competitive. For every success, hundreds of failed attempts at breaking in go unnoticed. But think positively and remain focused. If this is your passion, you *can* make it happen.

WHAT IS A SHORT FILM?

A feature-length film typically runs anywhere from ninety minutes to two-and-a-half hours. Occasionally they will play even longer. (Has anyone seen *Titanic*?) Obviously, a short film is shorter than a feature. Short films can be anywhere from thirty seconds to thirty minutes long, sometimes longer. "You have people who make twenty-minute shorts, even forty-five-minute shorts," says producer Steve Hein, a partner at Quality Films and a producer of several films that have successfully launched Hollywood careers, including *Battle of the Sexes* and *Inside.* "They're more 'mediums' than 'shorts.'"

That said, Hein feels the best length for a short is under ten minutes. "You're making a short to demonstrate that you can direct," says Hein. "If you can't demonstrate that you can direct in under ten minutes, you're probably running around in circles."

"I don't think you want to extend your short film adding a lot of stuff that is unnecessary to tell a story, because people get bored," says Eduardo Rodriguez, who directed a short film called *Daughter* that garnered him a three-picture deal with Dimension Films. "When you go out to see a short film, you want to see something that has a beginning, a middle, and an end in a very short time. You want to get something out of it—either a lesson, or a laugh, or a scary beat, whatever it is. You want to get it like a joke. I tell you this, and you have a reaction. That should determine the length of the short film. Whatever it takes you to tell that joke."

However, sometimes the story, not the form, dictates the length of a short film. "The script and the story you're trying to tell will ultimately tell you how long your film should be," says producer Gary Bryman, another partner and producer at Quality Films. "The 2001 Academy Award–winning short film was *The Accountant*—it was a thirty-five-minute film. It goes against conventional logic (the shorter the better), but it was exactly the length it needed to be to be as effective as it was."

WHAT MAKES A GREAT SHORT FILM?

Jana Sue Memel is a prolific producer of short films. Her shorts have been nominated for a total of eleven Academy Awards and have won three Oscars for Best Live Action Short. Memel says the same parameters that make a great feature make a great short.

"A short is just a long film—shorter," says Memel. "It should have all the elements of a good movie, which are a brilliant script, brilliant performances, fabulous camera work, great editing, and great music. I think story telling is harder [in a short film] because it's harder to have a beginning, middle, and end in less amount of pages. But when I'm watching a short, I am intrigued and engrossed by the ones where I cared about the characters and I wanted to know what would happen to them next, just like a feature film."

"What makes a good short film is that X factor that makes it rise above the clutter," says Gene Klein, vice president of acquisitions at Hypnotic Films. Klein watches thousands of shorts every year, and he says there are many that are very good. "A film can be very good by virtue of the quality of its writing, the quality of the production. But the best short films have something that makes them memorable. Sometimes memorable comes from a great punch line at the end of the film—and I'm not talking necessarily about a comedic punch line—so that you're leaving your audience with something at the end. The best short films are the ones that go for it, that tell unusual stories, that develop unusual characters, or that take a chance and come straight from the heart."

MAKING A SHORT FILM

There is not much money to be made from short films, although a few have proven themselves profitable. Rarely do shorts receive a theatrical release. And unless time and effort are taken to seek out these short films, most people never see them. That said, for a filmmaker, there are many reasons to make a short film.

- *Experience.* Filmmaking is like playing an instrument. The more you practice the piano, the better you get. The more film you shoot, the further you grow as a director. This book will talk a lot about making the definitive short, but that does not prevent you from picking up a video camera to shoot whenever you get the opportunity. Practice makes perfect. The more you can experience filmmaking at any level, the more prepared you will be to step behind the camera to make the piece that will launch your career.

- *Representation.* In order to procure an agent or manager, you will need something to show them. Although you would like to present them the best possible sample of your work, they might be able to evaluate your talent upon seeing a collection of more experimental pieces or student films.

- *Employment.* Having a short will show hiring entities what you are capable of. Producers and executives can view your work. If they respond positively to it, they might approach you to direct a project for them.

"When you make a short film you want it to demonstrate a handful of things," says Gary Bryman. "One, that you're a writer, because I think when executives are looking at young filmmakers, for the most part, they are looking for writer/directors. You want to show that you can also direct."

"Some people really enjoy the short form," says AtomFilms CEO, Mika Salmi. "That has increased in the United States. Some directors have made it now because they've established themselves in features or other media and they say I want to make a short because I really like the format. Now you're seeing the growth of advertisers using the short format as kind of an extended TV commercial with more of a narrative sense, whether it be BMW films, or on our site now we have Skyy Vodka and Honda. Hundreds of companies have done these now."

There are many reasons to make a short film, according to Salmi. "Sometimes it's a student project, so it's something you have to do to graduate. Other times, it's a résumé buffer. You need it in your reel. If you do television commercials, you also need a short to complement your reel. Or if you're a music video director, you need something on there to round it out to show that you can also do a narrative." Finally, Salmi notes that a good short film can act as a résumé or springboard of sorts for filmmakers hoping to break into the "holy grail" of feature films. "It tends to be a calling card," he says.

THE CALLING CARD

When I meet a potential business contact, I give him or her my business card. A head shot is an actor's business card. A writer has a script. A director has a reel.

A reel is a collection of scenes from various projects edited together to showcase a director's work. But if a director has nothing to edit together, or if the overall quality of what he has available just is not professional in nature, he might as well have nothing to show.

A short film can be a beginning director's calling card. If it makes a great impression, that short alone can lead to tremendous opportunities. This book will help you prepare the best calling card possible by showing you how other young filmmakers navigated the Hollywood system, armed only with their short and their passion, and ultimately found enough success to launch their careers.

"People want to become the next Steven Spielberg," says Adam Stein, executive vice president of IFilm, a website that showcases the work of short filmmakers. "There's a long list of talent out in the marketplace today that brings a variety of life experiences to the art of storytelling, and short filmmaking is a great way to produce a calling card for less money than it actually costs to put a feature film together. There are clearly those people who want to have a career as a director, producer, or writer, and short films provide them with a vehicle to get noticed in the marketplace."

Trevor Sands made a short for one reason. "The purpose was to create a sample of my work to showcase what I was capable of as a director to help me get a feature project off the ground—either one that I had written or a studio project that was open as a directing assignment," says Sands. "I had seen friends and colleagues of mine make shorts and have varying degrees of success over the years, and I had decided that it was a worthwhile investment for me as long as I had the right idea to go ahead and spend the money and do it right in hopes that it would pay off." After completing his short film *Inside,* Sands received a two-picture deal from Dimension Films. Now that is a rather satisfying payoff!

GETTING STARTED

People often ask me how to become a director. It might surprise you to find that there is really only one answer to that question. Direct a film.

Think about it. How does someone become a screenwriter? They write a script. Whether the screenplay sells or not, once they have written a script, they are a screenwriter all the same.

Hollywood careers are not like most other professions. To become a doctor you must first go to medical school. To become a lawyer, a J.D. is necessary. Sure, you can go to film school to learn the craft of directing, but until you actually direct something you are nothing more than a film school graduate. And unlike the professions previously mentioned, you do not *need* to get a degree to be a director. You just have to do it.

"I'm a big believer in learning by doing," says filmmaker Eric Kripke, who directed the short films *Truly Committed* and *Battle of the Sexes*. "Filmmaking is a craft. It's not like law. It's a craft as much as carpentry. It would be like going to carpentry school and having professors lecture about carpentry rather than just going off and building something."

"Making a short film is more valuable than four years of film school," says director Mike Mitchell. "One year of making your own film, especially when you pay for it yourself, makes you respect both ends of it."

For many who dream of a career in movies, the ultimate goal is to become a "filmmaker." But what exactly is a filmmaker?

In its simplest definition, a filmmaker is someone who makes films. Does this also include someone who makes TV programs? Is the "filmmaker" strictly the director? Or would an editor also be considered a filmmaker for all his hard work cutting together the film? What about a producer who puts together the project from beginning to end?

Although anyone working in the visual media can certainly consider him- or herself a filmmaker, for the purpose of this book, I will focus on the director as filmmaker. As you will see, although everyone else working on a short might walk away with a nice clip for their reel, it is really the director who receives recognition when the film is a success.

"Short films are a directors' medium," says Steve Hein. "Nobody's gonna be, 'Oh that short film is so well written,' because there are different rules that apply. With feature writing and television writing, there's such a structure to it. And with shorts, there's absolutely no structure to it."

Of course, very few people become directors right from the start. There are many other ways to gain experience that will help you later in your career when you are directing. In fact, many of today's top directors first found success in another craft. Getting started in each of these positions is very similar.

For most crew positions, you can start as an apprentice or assistant, learn the craft, and climb the ladder within the department. Many have successfully transitioned from apprentice editor to assistant editor to editor, or from film loader to camera assistant to camera operator to director of photography.

Even if you start as a Directors Guild trainee, you then become a second assistant director, first assistant director, and ultimately a production manager. But ironically, this program does not prepare you to become a director. Look at many of today's successful directors. Ron Howard (*A Beautiful Mind*) started his Hollywood career as an actor. Jan De Bont (*Speed*) began as a cinematographer. Robert Wise (*West Side Story*) got his start as an editor.

You can also springboard to a film career from another medium. Plenty of successful feature directors began their careers directing television (Joel Zwick), commercials (Charles Stone III), and music videos (Michael Bay). They can even come from the stage (Sam Mendes). Still, for a majority of today's filmmakers, the path to becoming a director leads through film school.

THE CASE FOR (AND AGAINST) FILM SCHOOL

Trevor Sands grew up in Gig Harbor, Washington, about an hour south of Seattle. He got interested in filmmaking very early on, starting out on a Super 8 camera and eventually graduating to an early camcorder. "I was the cool kid on the block because I had one of those portable VCRs with a strap," says Sands, who eventually shot more and more video because Super 8 just got too expensive. All through middle school and high school he burned hours of videotape shooting various shorts.

A fan of everything Spielberg, from second to fourth grade, Sands went to school every day dressed like Indiana Jones, complete with a whip. After seeing *Star Wars,* which was the first movie he saw in a theater, Sands announced that he wanted to go to film school. Even as a child, he was writing feature screenplays and making active plans to make that happen.

"The most valuable thing that came out of that era is the genuine spirit of creating for the sake of creating and having fun with it and not really getting bogged down with the rules and all the choices that would factor into making a short film that you're spending a tremendous amount of money on and that you want to really get serious results from," says Sands. "There's great value to the 'have fun with it' attitude."

"You go to film school to make films and to find out if you know what you're doing," says Joe Nussbaum. "There's nothing like having a room full of people tell you that they didn't understand what happened in your short. You better go back and make it coherent."

"The world that I know stands on the back of a single short film that you make when you're young," says animation director Peter Lord. "In film school somebody makes a movie. There's something about that age, there's something about the freedom of being at film school, something about the philosophy that runs through film school that encourages experimentation. People come up with films that are very personal, very unique, and have a very strong identity. If you can do that, your career then stands on the back of your film and is launched by that film. And if you miss that chance, it's very difficult to make a career in short films. In my life, I've met other very talented animators who've never had a film in their name where they're the auteur. They can make a successful career as an animator, but not as a director or filmmaker."

"If you want to go to film school, go. You can go anywhere," says writer/director Eric Kripke, a USC [University of Southern California] graduate. "It doesn't matter what school you go to. What matters is getting on set and shooting. You can talk about art, and it's good to learn, but when you're on set and you're losing light and your actors aren't ready, you need to improvise, and you need to be creative and smart and clever and relaxed.

"It's like catching butterflies at a construction site," continues Kripke. "You're trying to capture this one piece of beauty surrounded in the middle of loud, angry, sharp edges everywhere. When it's your own money burning away, it's a great way to learn because the pressure is so heavy. And you'll learn a lot more about cutting by cutting yourself. And you'll learn a lot more about performance by directing performance yourself. You learn much, much more than anything you'll ever learn inside a classroom."

Long before Luke Greenfield directed such big features as *The Animal* and *The Girl Next Door*, he, too, studied filmmaking at USC. He found film school to be extremely competitive. "USC is like a movie studio," says Greenfield. "In the undergraduate program, you had to compete against everyone to make a sixteen-millimeter, sync-sound film that will be presented to the industry."

I don't mean to give film school a bad rap. In fact, it's just the opposite. Some of the best and brightest talent comes out of film schools. It's the best place to get educated about the filmmaking process.

But it is important to have a clear understanding of what film school will prepare you to do. Rarely is someone handed a movie to direct upon graduation from film school. This would only be the case if they came out of film school with an incredible short film, and they got it in front of the right people. And although I have seen some real winning student films from various film programs, the best shorts I have seen have actually come from film school graduates who have a few more years of experience under their belts.

Greenfield admits that some amazing things came out of his experience at film school, such as the connections. "USC is so in-tune with the industry," says Greenfield. "The agents *do* come to your screening. That was how my first step into the business worked."

Fellow USC graduate Trevor Sands agrees. "The best part of film school, without question, was the students, the people I met there, and the

LETTER OF ADMISSION

Long before he found success as the director of such films as *The Animal* and *The Girl Next Door,* Luke Greenfield grew up as an only child in Connecticut. Having had no siblings to play with, he found hobbies he could do alone. He began to draw and aspired to be an artist. And although he had a very strong imagination, he could not draw very well.

When Greenfield was ten, his uncle gave him a Super 8 camera. He quickly began making all sorts of experimental short films. He loved it. He would have screenings for his friends and family, and as he grew and gained more experience, his films got bigger and more ambitious. By the time he got to high school, he was making hour-long movies.

Like many aspiring filmmakers, Greenfield was obsessed with Steven Spielberg. He researched everything he could about the director of classics such as *ET: The Extra Terrestrial* and *Jaws.* Amidst his research, Greenfield discovered that Spielberg had always wanted to go to USC. He immediately began to learn as much about the school as possible, and he became obsessed with getting into the USC film program.

"I worried about the future," admits Greenfield. "I wanted to make sure I got into USC and became Steven Spielberg by age twenty-one. That was the whole goal."

Greenfield wrote letters to David Johnson, who was then head of the production department at the university. "I would write this guy letters every three months, and he didn't respond for a year," recalls Greenfield. "At the time, I was only twelve or thirteen! I didn't know how to spell 'admissions.' I wrote 'Dean of Emissions.' I kept sending him videotape copies of my Super 8 movies. Finally he responded."

By the time Greenfield was old enough to apply to USC film school, the faculty all knew him there. "I was the kid who had been writing letters for the past five years."

Greenfield was waiting patiently to receive his acceptance letter when he got a random phone call from a woman who asked if he would guarantee he'd come to USC if they gave him a scholarship. Greenfield asked if that meant he was in. "She said, 'Oh yeah, you're in,' and that's how I found out," says Greenfield. "For a couple days, my parents and I thought it was a crank call."

environment that's created when lots of people who love movies get together," says Sands. "It's a training ground to learn how people talk about movies and to develop relationships that for me have become very valuable. I still have great friends from my time at USC who have had a big influence on me in my career."

THE PURPOSE OF THIS BOOK

Whether you went to film school or learned to make movies on your own, this book will help you focus your talent and skills to create effective short films. There are plenty of books that teach you how to make a film. All the principles that apply to making a feature also apply to making a short. The emphasis of this book will be those issues that are unique to making a short film.

Remember, this book is less of a step-by-step how-to of physically making a short, and more of a theoretical look at how making the right short can launch your career. This is not a substitute for film school or for actually making a movie. Still, you will find plenty of valuable advice on how to put together a short film.

You are now ready to continue this journey. However, before you reach for your camera, it is imperative to have a well-thought-out idea for the short film you wish to make. The next chapter will aid you in coming up with a winning concept.

2

> "I've always thought the short form is a lot more fun. It fits my attention span: It's quicker, it's tighter, it can be more interesting and a little more daring or innovative than a feature, not necessarily in technique, but in story line and subject matter."
>
> —Mika Salmi, CEO, AtomFilms

GEORGE LUCAS IN LOVE

Being that movies are very much a collaborative effort, Joe Nussbaum had a little help with his short film. Nussbaum first met Joseph Levy at USC's freshman barbecue, and the two became fast friends. Although Levy was a music major, he worked in the film school's operations office and desired a career in the movie business. Levy was aching to produce a short film when he first approached Nussbaum with the notion. But they did not yet have a story concept.

Tim Dowling, a theater major, was another USC pal. He and Nussbaum were members of the same improv comedy troupe, Commedus Interruptus. "Tim was the little bird in my ear that kept saying, 'You have to make a parody. If you want to get known, this is what you have to do,'" says Nussbaum.

Tim suggested that *Shakespeare in Love* was the movie Nussbaum and

Levy should parody. His initial idea was to call it *Joe Eszterhas in Love* after the screenwriter of films such as *Basic Instinct* and *Showgirls*. "It can be the antithesis of *Shakespeare*," says Nussbaum. "How did this dirty old man who writes nothing but nasty, bitter, sexual, tawdry stuff find his inspiration? It could be very funny." But ultimately, Nussbaum decided that this was not the film he wanted to make.

Then the team came up with the idea of *Stephen King in Love*. "Just normal Stephen King before he's ever written anything and he's got a vicious dog named Cujo and a car that has a mind of its own," says Nussbaum. "Stephen King is a hugely successful author, but I don't really think he resonates on a personal level with too many people, and certainly not with me."

The guys continued to brainstorm ideas. At the time, there was a lot of hype surrounding the impending release of *Star Wars: Episode I—The Phantom Menace*. Inspiration hit Nussbaum stronger than a Jedi mind trick. "I loved *Star Wars*. *Star Wars* was my childhood. I had every toy. I knew the movie backward and forward. Tim was the same way."

Dowling and Nussbaum beat out a story about how George Lucas found his inspiration for *Star Wars*. Next, Nussbaum wrote an outline and gave it to another buddy, Dan Shere. Nussbaum had known Shere for more than fifteen years. The two had gone to summer camp together when they were boys. Shere wrote a draft of the script. Then Shere and Nussbaum rewrote and tweaked until they had a six-and-a-half-page script that they called *George Lucas in Love*.

This chapter will assist you in coming up with your own great story for a short film. First I will discuss the various formats of short films. Then I will help you choose a genre to work in. Finally, I will examine where to find inspiration and ideas for the films you wish to make.

FORMAT

When coming up with an idea for your short film, there are certain factors you must consider. To begin with, what type of short will you make?

There are four basic formats: narrative, documentary, animation, and experimental.

Narrative films tell a story. They have a beginning, middle, and end. Most feature films you see are narrative in structure. But telling a story in under ten minutes can prove quite challenging. That is why these shorts tend to be scripted and well planned out. *George Lucas in Love* is an example of a narrative short.

Documentary shorts analyze true events with little or no fictionalization. They tend to combine interviews with footage of real events. And although lots of preparation takes place to set up interview subjects and request permission to film live events, these films typically come together in the editing room. *Twin Towers,* a film about September 11, 2001, was an Academy Award–winning documentary short in 2002.

Animated shorts are generally narrative in style. They stand apart from the rest because they usually consist of photographing a series of drawings or inanimate objects each showing a slight movement from the one before so they appear to be moving when they are projected back to an audience. Audiences might recall the animated short *For the Birds,* which played in theaters before the animated feature *Monsters, Inc.* Occasionally, shorts will combine animation and live-action together like *Bed and Breakfast.*

A fourth type of short is the **experimental** short. These films tend to combine elements of the other three types of film, although they generally do not tell a narrative story and tend to be more visual in nature. If you are making a short with the aim of launching your career, experimental shorts are less likely to achieve this goal. However, if you are making experimental shorts to try new techniques and grow as a filmmaker before you prepare your calling card, they can be very productive. *Begone Dull Care* is an example of an experimental short film in which the filmmaker painted abstract shapes and colors directly on the filmstrip, which shifted to variations of music.

Of course, there are always exceptions. Take Peter Lord, one of the most successful men working in animation today. Before directing the animated feature *Chicken Run* with partner Nick Park, his Aardman Studios had won five Academy Awards for Best Animated Short. Lord also started his career with one short film, *Down and Out,* which had a fairly unique concept. "The idea goes way back to John and Faith Hubley, two American experimental filmmakers in the late 1950s who made an animated film using the voices of their children," explains Lord. "They recorded their children telling a story and then they animated to match the story the children were telling."

No children were used in Lord's film, but he did use real soundtracks. "We went to a Salvation Army hostel with a tape recorder, hid somewhere, and recorded the dialogue that went on as guys came in and wanted a bed for the night or a meal," says Lord. "We took five minutes of that, edited it quite substantially, and made a film based on it. What we had was a very real voice track, very simple everyday kind of conversation, but with a certain natural drama in what was happening, and then crudely made animation, modeling clay figures, appearing to speak the lines. That particular crossover between a documentary approach using very naturalistic soundtrack and close observation of human mannerisms is the magic formula that we're still using today."

Choose a format for your short film that you wish to use as a feature director. If you want to become the next Michael Moore, make a documentary short. If you want to become the next Steven Spielberg, a narrative short is in order. Once you decide which format you will be working in, you must then decide what genre to focus on.

GENRE

The genre is the type of film you wish to make, whether it be comedy, drama, action, thriller, horror, musical, etc. It is an important decision. If your short film is well received by Hollywood, you might be given a chance to direct at the professional level. But this opportunity will be very specific. If you have proven that you are adept to direct comedy, then comedy is what you will be hired to direct. If you really want to be directing thrillers, then you must prove that you are capable of handling this kind of material and, therefore, that is the kind of short you should make.

It works the same way in the professional arena. Wes Craven makes horror films. John Landis directs comedies. David Fincher is known for his thrillers. Is that to say these talented directors could not direct something outside the genre for which they are known? Of course not. But it is a challenge, and Hollywood would much prefer to have them continue to direct what they have already proven time and again they are great at.

You might be apprehensive about this train of thought. You do not want to be stereotyped. This is understandable, but the reality is, especially when starting out, that you *need* to be labeled. You must be known for something (whether that something is directing comedies, directing musicals, etc.) and for doing it well. Studio executives need these labels for directors—the same way they need them for actors or anyone else in the business. Tom Hanks, Robin Williams, and Jim Carey all began as "the funny guy." As their careers evolved, they were able to cross over into other types of roles. Directing careers develop the same way.

My philosophy in managing careers of writers and directors follows a similar train of thought. The first thing I want to do is put someone in a box. If you direct comedies, I want you to focus only on comedies. I want to introduce you to the town as a comedy director. And I want you to establish yourself professionally as a person who directs comedies. When studios are looking to hire a director for their next comedy, I want your name to be on the top of the list.

But once you are firmly established in that box, I want to work twice as hard to get you out of that genre. Sure, you can direct comedies—you do it better than anyone else. But you also have an eye for drama. It might take some time to help you transition out of that box, so choose a genre you are completely comfortable with and wanting to work in when you first establish your career. If you do good work and make smart choices, you will eventually be able to direct whatever type of material you want. Remember, once you have attained a certain level of success, you will have also gained some power to call your shots.

SPOOF OF LIFE

Spoofs can be a great way to grab Hollywood's attention. But like any story idea, make sure your spoof is unique and original. When *The Blair Witch Project* came out, it inspired a slew of parodies. "There were literally about fifteen *Blair Witch* parodies floating around town," says Joe Nussbaum. "It was so easy to spoof because the whole look of *Blair Witch* was home video."

Nussbaum actually read an article in the *LA Times* about a guy who saw *The Blair Witch Project* one night, went home, wrote a parody of it, shot it the next day, and had it around town two days later. But because of the sheer number of similar spoofs, short films on this topic had a tough time getting noticed. "That was the death of these films," says Nussbaum. "I think when the fifteenth *Blair Witch* parody hit the desk of Joe Executive, he was like, 'I don't care. I don't want to watch this.'

"What gets the short film in the VCR [of the film executive]? At the time we did it, it was being a spoof."

Let me offer you a word of caution: You cannot simply make what is "hot" at the moment. You also have to make a film that is true to you. In the best case, you will make a film that is commercial and comes from your passion.

Gary Bryman, producer of many short films, including *Inside* and *Battle of the Sexes,* agrees that it is important to pick a format and genre you want to be "known" for in your future work. "Be specific in the way you present yourself," he says. "If you make a horror piece, you'll be the horror guy. Don't make a horror short if you want to direct romantic comedies."

"Have a goal in mind when you set off to make your project if your long-term goal is to be a narrative feature film director," advises Bryman.

"But if you just have a story that's dying to be told and you just want to make it to make it, you don't need to be quite as focused or have quite a master game plan. If you're working within the Hollywood system, it's very important to give it a very deliberate attempt at making the types of movies you would like to direct. It's your calling card."

"I knew I wanted to do a comedy. And ultimately I wanted to do a comedy with some romance," says Joe Nussbaum, whose first short, *George Lucas in Love,* was, in fact, a romantic comedy. Not surprisingly, most of the films Nussbaum has been attached to in his professional career have either been true romantic comedies or comedies with some romantic elements.

"I have a friend who made a comedy spoof because that's what was getting noticed, but it really wasn't him. And in retrospect, I think he would have been a lot better served by doing a horror short or thriller short, because that's more him," continues Nussbaum. "But I wanted to do comedy, so for me it was the perfect choice.

"The nice thing about *George Lucas in Love,* as much as it is a parody, it has a little romance. That was important to me because it gave me a chance to have one or two nice scenes where I can show that I can make an actor and an actress connect."

WHAT'S THE BIG IDEA?

When asked what makes a great film, I always respond "a great story." The same is true for the short form. Whether it is a plot that is unique and different from everything else like it in the genre, a concept that has never before been explored, or a new twist on a familiar notion, everything else comes second to that one great idea.

With *George Lucas in Love,* Joe Nussbaum had the brilliant idea of fusing the feature film *Shakespeare in Love* with the world of George Lucas and *Star Wars.* Trevor Sands created a classic *Twilight Zone* twist in an original setting in *Inside.* You can come up with a great idea, too.

"I think a film has to look great and be an attention-grabber," admits Gary Bryman. "But if you've got just a bunch of good-looking visuals and there's no story there and there's no emotional connection with the audience, then to me it's a [music] video. So depending on the type of work the filmmaker is looking to do, if he wants to make a narrative feature film, and it is his goal to be directing those kinds of projects, it's important to have him tell a good story. It all starts on the page. It's the foundation from which everything else is going to come."

"I believe one of the things about first-time filmmaking is that the closer it is to you in your heart, the easier it is to make the film," says Oscar-winning short film producer Jana Sue Memel. "For all films, if it isn't on the page, it isn't on the screen. So it's really important to come up with an amazing story."

"If you're just looking to express yourself and have something to play in festivals, then go nuts," says Eric Kripke. "But if what you're trying to do is further your career and get jobs as a filmmaker, then there's nothing more important than the concept. You're trying to create a product, and in your four or five minutes you really need to hook somebody. And you need to demonstrate cleverness in a very short period of time, so a sharp concept is the best way to do that."

"A good short film is like a good movie is like a good piece of music. It's the story that's being told and how it is delivered to the audience," says IFilm's Adam Stein. "At the end of the day, when you strip away all the technology, the story being told really must be compelling, something that is moving and emotional—it makes you laugh, cry, or angry."

There are many different sources for story ideas. Feature films are based on a variety of underlying material. From books to TV shows, toys to comic books, newspaper articles to true-life events, great stories surround us. As a filmmaker, it is your job to identify these ideas and breathe life into them onscreen.

Ideas from Your Life

Finding that right piece of material is integral to your success. When you are at the level of Academy Award–winning producer Jana Sue Memel, great material finds you. "The material often comes from short stories that are incredibly hard to adapt, because what's good about a short story is generally internal and how to externalize that is often incredibly difficult," says Memel. "A lot of the shorts I've made, I've encouraged the people who have come to me and said they want to direct to write some form of something that comes out of their life, because most people lead far more interesting lives than any of us would think. And certainly a kernel of an episode of their life fictionalized would be great."

Bryan Gordon based his short film on a personal experience that came right out of working in Hollywood. "I had lunch with a couple agents, and they were being so familiar with me when I just didn't know who they were," explains Gordon. "One of them put their hand on my arm in a familiar way." Because Gordon barely knew the agent, it made him feel somewhat uncomfortable. That is when he came up with the silly idea, "Wouldn't it be nice if businessmen were in a room and they were simply asked to hold each other and dance to get ahead?"

Gordon wrote down that notion and put it aside. "I thought this would be a great short film," continues Gordon. "The story of a guy trying to get a job and the only thing he has to do was dance with other men in this heterosexual atmosphere to get ahead. It's as if Donald Trump said one day, 'Instead of taking me to lunch, just dance with me.' "

Ray's Male Heterosexual Dance Hall, which Gordon directed and Memel produced, went on to win the Academy Award for Best Live-Action Short. "I never thought it was a feature. What it was, was simply a short film," says Gordon. "When it came time to write the piece, I wanted to write something that was extremely succinct and short and containable because I think that's what short films have to be. They're basically really great short stories that have to be told in a very simple way."

Most, if not all documentary shorts come from life events. *Big Mama* is a documentary short about Viloa Dees, an elderly woman trying to take care of her troubled grandson. *One Survivor Remembers* tells the true story of Holocaust survivor Gerda Weissmann Klein and her memories both before and after the war. *If You Love This Planet* warns against the dangers of nuclear arms.

Ideas Adapted from Other Sources

It is not necessary to create an entirely original idea. When Eric Kripke was a child he had read a short story in *Twilight Zone Magazine* called "Truly Committed" by author Richard Matheson. He knew right then that one day he would make this story into a film. What he did not know were the challenges that lay ahead in securing the rights to the short story.

"We needed to secure the rights to this thing, but I went ahead and wrote the script anyway," says Kripke, describing one of the cardinal sins of moviemaking. "We were in pre-production and I contacted Richard Matheson's agent. 'Hello, I'm a college kid and I want the rights to this story.' And they were like 'No way.'" Kripke freaked out. He did not know what he was going to do. They could not shoot their movie without permission to use the underlying material.

He decided that whatever it took, he would track down the author and speak with him directly. For three weeks, Kripke researched Matheson, hoping to find another way to reach the author. "Nothing but slammed doors," remembers Kripke. Then he happened to go back to his hometown, where he visited the Toledo Lucas County Public Library. "I went up to the librarian and asked if there was any chance she might have any contact information for an author named Richard Matheson. She looked in her computer and said, 'I don't know if this is the guy, but we have an address in Woodland Hills.'"

Kripke took the address and wrote him a letter. "Dear Mr. Matheson, I've been a huge fan. We're making this movie. It's not for profit. It's based on your short story. We don't have any money. Please can we have the rights? I don't know if this is the right guy, but if it is, please help me," recites Kripke, who mailed the letter and continued moving forward with the project.

Seven weeks before the start of production, Kripke received a fax. "It was the letter I wrote to Woodland Hills, and scrawled at the bottom was 'I'll give you the rights. I won't charge you a dime. Good luck. R. Matheson,'" says Kripke. "The lesson here is get it done, no matter what. You can never give up and never quit. If you find an insurmountable obstacle, then you weren't meant to be making movies in the first place. The whole thing is about impossibility, so you have to be willing to conquer the impossible in every realm."

Ideas That Resonate

Eric Kripke was pleased with the final results of his first short film, *Truly Committed*. The film caught the attention of several agents and producers, but it did not catapult him to the next level. He continued to struggle as an aspiring filmmaker. Kripke did not let it get him down. The ever-ambitious director saved up some money and geared up for a second attempt.

Kripke and a group of his friends were sitting around one night, wildly inebriated, talking about girl trouble. "We had all been recently dumped one way or another," remembers Kripke. "We were all exchanging war stories, and eerie similarities started to emerge. Women had been using the same line and the same words. One guy, I think he cheated on his girlfriend in another state—no connection whatsoever—and then he came back and she was like, 'You cheated on me.' She knew!"

The friends started laughing, and at that moment, inspiration hit Kripke. I still have it in one of my notebooks scrawled in my drunk handwriting," continues Kripke. "Underground conspiracy of women." In the short film, a guy and a girl are on a date. When he asks her to come back to his place, she excuses herself to the ladies' room. Inside the rest room, a team of women with high-tech gadgetry assess her male companion. They alert the unsuspecting girl of what she would be in for (not a pretty picture) if she began a relationship with him, and she decides not to go home with the guy. The guy has no idea what hit him.

His friends helped Kripke shoot the short. And this time it did the trick. *Battle of the Sexes* became the calling card that *Truly Committed* was not able to be. "A lot of people seem to respond to it,'" says Kripke. "I think they were able to grab hold of it very easily. It was something that someone wanted to tell his or her friend about."

BATTLE OF THE SEXES
by Eric Kripke

FADE IN . . .

INT. BAR- NIGHT
It is a sight we've seen a million times: a guy picking up on a girl. MAX, 20s, sits at the bar. He's handsome, charm-ing and genuine. ANNIE, 20's, sits next to him. She's pretty and sweet.

Whatever he's been saying has clearly been effective. They make intense, direct eye contact.

    MAX: . . . before I say it, you gotta know, it's
    just . . . me going out at all is a Guiness Book event,
    much less hitting it off with . . . I should just say
    it, huh? Okay. Do you . . . why don't you come back to
    my place—ugh, <u>that's</u> such a "Love Boat" line, sorry.
    I just thought we'd stay up and keep talking, you
    know? I got a penthouse, got a great view, I'm not
    trying to brag or anything, I worked really hard for
    it. I just thought we'd be impulsive, maybe.

Annie's eyes sparkle— she's attracted to Max. For a beat or two, she stares into his eyes.

   ANNIE: I'm gonna run to the ladies room, okay?

She heads to the ladies room. Before she walks in, she turns around to look at Max. He flashes a killer smile. She meekly smiles back.

INT. LADIES BATHROOM- CONTINUOUS
Annie walks in, grinning to herself, positively enamored. She closes the bathroom door.

Suddenly, her expression changes. No more goofy romance— she's steely-eyed, all business.

   ANNIE: I need a background check!

There are several WOMEN in the bathroom, checking their make-up, gossiping, etc. In a split second, they're all business as well.

A RED LIGHT FLASHES. THE WOMEN TAKE THEIR BATTLE STATIONS, STAND BEHIND HIDDEN COMPUTER CONSOLES THAT SPRING FROM THE WALLS, SINKS, ETC.

The following events should have the military pacing and feel of a submarine mission, or the crew of the starship En- terprise as they're heading into battle . . .

CUE- POUNDING, ACTION MOVIE-TYPE MUSIC
Annie sits down on the toilet. A DECK COMPUTER LOWERS FROM THE CEILING. She TAPS the keys like a professional hacker.

COMPUTER: Must return in three minutes . . .

ON THE COMPUTER SCREEN
MAX'S FACE MATERIALIZES, with STATISTICS RAPIDLY FILING DOWN
THE SCREEN.

ANNIE (calling out): Physical stats!?

AT THE BATHROOM SINK
A BLONDE reads a COMPUTER DATA SHEET that spits from a MAXI-
PAD VENDING MACHINE.

SHANTI: Physical stats! Back Hair— predominant.

A YOUNG ROOKIE stands close by, reading a monitor.

MONIQUE: He's gassy.

Another WOMAN whizzes past on a rolling chair.

LALANYA: Genitalia size— way below average.

Annie crisply nods.

ANNIE: Behavior!?

AT ANOTHER CORNER OF THE BATHROOM
An ELDERLY WOMAN presses her eyes into the same viewfinder
thing that Mr. Spock used.

LIZ: Behavior! He lied about usually staying home—he
spends most of his time at strip bars.

ANNIE: Employment status!?

AT ANOTHER CORNER
A printer spits out a picture of Max. Next to the printer, the rookie works feverently on a computer.

MONIQUE (to herself): Earning potential— low.

The tension mounts— it's taking too long.

COMPUTER: One minute warning . . .

ANNIE: Employment status!? Come on— what's the man's job!!?

All eyes are on the rookie. Sweat pours down her brow.

MONIQUE (mutters): Oh, my God . . . (calling out with desperation) He's a plumber! Repeat, he's a plumber!

INT. BAR- CONTINUOUS
Max waits at the bar, clueless to just about everything. "THE GIRL FROM IMPANEMA" plays on the jukebox. He waves to a WAITRESS, but she doesn't see him. He self-consciously transforms the wave into brushing back his hair.

HIDDEN POV
We spy Max through the CROSS-HAIRS of some kind of SCOPE. He secretly picks his nose.

INT. LADIES BATHROOM- CONTINUOUS
ANOTHER WOMAN keeps an eye on Max through a submarine-style PERISCOPE.

ELIZABETH: We gotta nose picker . . .

Lalanya studies her computer console.

LALANYA: Wait . . . he doesn't live in a Penthouse! He lives in his parents' attic!

Annie, sitting behind her computer on the toilet, nods.

ANNIE: Consensus?

ELIZABETH: Negative.

LIZ: Negative.

MONIQUE: Negative.

LALANYA: Negative.

SHANTI: Negative.

ANNIE: Thank you, ladies.

INT. BAR- MINUTES LATER
Annie, all sugar and spice again, finishes up her conversation with Max.

MAX: Are you sure? I'm telling you, you don't know what you're missing . . .

ANNIE: I think I do. Sorry.

ON A VIDEO SCREEN
We watch Max walk away from Annie, broken, defeated, and confused about where things went south.

```
INT. LADIES BATHROOM- CONTINUOUS
HIGH ANGLE
Looking down on all the LADIES (with several more EXTRAS as
well) as they stare up at the CLOSED-CIRCUIT TELEVISION
mounted high on the bathroom wall.

THEY ALL CHEER! It should remind you of mission control af-
ter a safe and successful space shuttle flight.

Lalanya stands next to the wise Elderly Woman. They keep
their eyes glued to the monitor as they speak.


     LALANYA: Men . . .

     LIZ (matter-of-factly) They're all just a bunch of
     bitches . . .

                              SMASH CUT TO BLACK

FIN
```

Ideas Carefully Calculated to Get You Hired

Trevor Sands was not fooling around. He had produced a low-budget straight-to-video feature while he was still a student at USC. But for all his hard work, he still could not get arrested as a feature director. So he went back to the drawing board to create a new calling card that would help elevate him to that next level.

He wanted to direct a movie that was less than ten minutes. "I've seen short films that are successful that are a half-hour, but in my experience—particularly if your goal is to use it as a calling card—people don't want to spend much longer than that watching a short film," says Sands. "And then if you can give something to them that is impressive in that amount of time, they will appreciate you more than if you make them spend a half-hour and give them something that is mediocre or might not hit every mark."

Sands also decided that he wanted to do something that was self-contained and not too ambitious. He wanted to shoot it the way a studio feature is shot. That meant it had to take place in a room and it could not be very effects-intensive because he was not prepared to spend half a million dollars to make this film.

Sands knew he did not want to direct a comedy because the features he wanted to make were not comedies. "I knew that whatever short film you make is what they will think of you as," says Sands. "If you don't want to be a comedy director, don't shoot a comedy short. Problem is, the best shorts are comedies because of the setup—punch line—joke kind of structure. Short and sweet, in and out, cute and clever—it's that simple. Whereas to do a drama, you don't have time to develop character and do what you have to do to make a drama effective. It's not conducive to the short format."

Sands also did not want to make a film that was too esoteric. "As much as I can appreciate those kinds of movies, I don't think studio executives do," says Sands. "You can have something that might be very impressive visually and doing something you think has artistic integrity and might be cutting-edge or more interesting than your average fare, but I had hung out in the Hollywood community long enough to know that that's not necessarily appreciated and doesn't necessarily apply to what they're looking for when it comes to making a feature film, which is the ability to tell a clear story."

Ultimately, Sands decided to make something in the vein of *The Twilight Zone*. "When I thought about it, those were probably some of the best short films ever made," says Sands.

Sands knew that if he had a *Twilight Zone*–type twist at the end of his film, the audience would be both satisfied and surprised. "From that came the idea to do something cinematically involving performances around the concept of multiple personality disorder and using the alters as characters in a scene speaking through and in syncopation with the main character," says Sands. "I thought that was very interesting and unique and would serve my desire to do something impressive, but that it would also provide an opportunity to tell a clear story." In fact, as you can see from the script on the following pages, Sands succeeded. *Inside* has a clear act structure, a clear beginning and end, a clear main character, and a clever twist at the end. More important, the finished film did its part in elevating the young filmmaker to the next level of his career. Dimension Films gave Sands a two-picture deal: to write one film and direct another.

```
                        INSIDE
             by Trevor Sands & Eric Giz Gewirtz

From BLACK we PULL BACK to REVEAL

AN EYE.

We continue to PULL BACK to REVEAL

DANIEL. Age 29. Scruffy and untamed, sitting on the floor
of a PADDED CELL.

As we WIDEN we notice a group of PEOPLE gathered around him.
Some stand, some sit. Others pace nervously. All seem oddly
out of place as details of their character are revealed
through shadows:

A seven year old girl, BETH, eyes wide with fear. Her white
sundress is dirty and tattered.
A balding overweight man, OWEN, face in his hands.
A sad looking middle aged woman, MISS MARY WRIGHT, greying
hair tied up in a bun.
```

A tall skinny man with a manic look, PIERCE. Hair is long and he is covered in tattoos.

BO is a musclebound brute, jaw tight.

JOEY is a glossy-eyed guy in a wrinkled suit.

An elderly gray-haired man in a sweater, POPS.

HARRIS is hunched over, fidgety, mumbling to himself.

Hold on the high angle view of this madman and his surreal companions . . .

                                            FADE TO BLACK.

INSIDE

                                            FADE UP ON:

A blurry SQUARE. It holds, and we deduce through the soft focus we are looking at a white door with a small wire-laced window. After a beat, there is a CLANK and the SHA-SHINK of lock and key. The door OPENS. An ORDERLY steps forward and his face COMES INTO FOCUS.

    ORDERLY: On your feet. Doctor wants to see you.

Daniel looks up from his contorted position on the floor.

Orderly grabs his arm and hoists him up.

    ORDERLY: Let's go, I said. No trouble now.

Orderly guides a queasy-looking Daniel out of the PADDED CELL, where another ORDERLY is waiting. The door is closed behind them with a decisive CLANG.

INT. HALLWAY

MOVING with Daniel and the Orderlies down a glossy-floored hospital hallway. We PAN left to reveal BETH, the little girl, walking next to them— skipping, actually to keep up with their strides.

    DR. JANE (V.O.): Now, I've met Beth . . .

PAN right to reveal OWEN walking with them, head down.

    DR. JANE (V.O.): Owen . . .

PAN right to reveal MISS MARY WRIGHT, in place of young Beth. She checks her watch.

    DR. JANE (V.O.): Mary . . .

Pace faster. Quick PAN left to REVEAL strongman BO.

    DR. JANE (V.O.): And Bo.

INT. INTERVIEW ROOM

DR. JANE sits at a table. She is dressed in a white lab coat, middle aged— a strong woman with a strange presence.

    DR. JANE: Pops, Harris, Joey, and Pierce . . .

REVEAL Daniel, sitting across from her, flanked by his group of ALTERS (the doctor does not acknowledge them): BETH, OWEN, MISS WRIGHT, BO, and PIERCE.

    DR. JANE: Weeks now we've been talking, and you've introduced me to a lot of different people, each with a different name. So, my question is: who am I speaking to now?

Behind Daniel, the Alters speak up:

PIERCE: She's one of them. Don't trust her.

BETH: Why is that lady here?

OWEN: Who cares? It won't make any difference anyway.

MISS WRIGHT: She's here to help us.

BO charges up to the table, red-faced. When Daniel speaks, one of the Alters always SPEAKS THROUGH HIM, meaning they speak AT THE SAME TIME.

DANIEL/BO: THAT DOESN'T MATTER! What matters is HOW DO I GET OUT OF THIS PLACE!?

Daniel LUNGES, but the restraints have him pinned. Bo whirls and POUNDS on the wall madly. Dr. Jane remains perfectly calm, apparently unaware the Alters are present.

MISS WRIGHT (to Bo): Use your Indoor voice young man, this is a civilized place!

PIERCE: Intimidation won't work. She's one of them, inside my head— bugs in the system. Bad, bad vibes.

OWEN: Give it a rest already.

BETH: Don't be mean.

DR. JANE: Next week, you're up for evaluation. If it goes well, you'll qualify for a supervised release program, and eventually— parole. If you'll calm down and work with me, I can help make sure that happens.

DANIEL/MISS WRIGHT: I'm so sorry doctor. I've done horrible things. Terrible, terrible things. I want to change. Set things right.

PIERCE: Deny everything, confess nothing, she's trying to trick us!

BO (screams at Doctor): I'LL TEAR YOUR HEAD OFF!

OWEN: Oh God, when is this going to end?

BETH: I saw him do the bad things.

DR. JANE: It's good you want to change, but you're suffering from a condition known as dissociative identity disorder— multiple personalities. You can only get better if—

DANIEL/PIERCE: You work for the government! You're inside my head. You can read my thoughts. I'm being held here against my will!

DR. JANE: You're here because the alternate selves inside your head have taken control. I can help you reclaim your true identity. But in order to do that, I need to know your real name.

DANIEL/OWEN: My name doesn't matter. None of this matters. Just let me die. I'm not important.

DR. JANE: You are important, and your name is important. Your name represents your individuality, your sense of self. Without a name, you can't know who you really are.

We hear EERIE LAUGHTER, and soon a new alter known as JOEY strolls onto the scene, giddy in a haunting "not quite sane" fashion.

> DANIEL/JOEY (eerie laugh): That's hilarious! I don't think I ever heard something so FUNNY!

Veins pop out on Daniel's head as he forces a loud, disturbing laugh. Young Beth steps up timidly.

> DANIEL/BETH: Mommy, can I go outside and play?
>
> DR. JANE: Is this Beth?
>
> DANIEL/PIERCE: No.
>
> DR. JANE: Pierce?
>
> DANIEL/PIERCE (mocking her): Guess again.
>
> DR. JANE: Who is this then?
>
> DANIEL/BO: I know who I am!
>
> DR. JANE: Then tell me.

HARRIS parades onto the scene, SINGING loudly:

> DANIEL/HARRIS <u>John Jacob Jingle Heimer Schmidt! Thaa-at's my name too!</u>

> BO: NO SINGING! I HATE THAT SONG!
>
> PIERCE: We're unravelling. Keep it together.

JOEY (laughing): You guys are a RIOT!

HARRIS: <u>Whenever we go out, the people always shout, "There goes Jingle Heimer Schmidt!"</u> <u>DA-DA-DADA-DADADA!</u>

DANIEL/BO: Too crowded in here, too much noise. Can't think straight. STOP TALKING!

Old man POPS hobbles onto the scene, scolding.

DANIEL/POPS: I told you we'd end up here. Never amount to nothin', never have never will.

PIERCE: Show no weakness!

MISS WRIGHT: Can't we all just get along?

OWEN: Why not!? We ARE weak! We're worthless!

BETH (singing): <u>Row, row, row your boat, gently down the stream . . .</u>

DR. JANE: When you were a child, what did your parents call you?

DANIEL/BETH (singing): <u>Merrily, merrily, merrily, merrily, life is but a D!</u>

DR. JANE: You said "D." Does your name start with a "D"?

DANIEL/BETH: B is for Boy, C is for Cat, D is for . . .

DR. JANE: D is for what? What is D for?

Daniel blinks several times, struggling with something deep inside himself. The VOICES around him rise to a PEAK as we MOVE around the room:

BO: Chatter-chatter-talk-talk-talk, ENOUGH TALK! I WANT OUT, NOW!

POPS: You good for nothin' waste of space. Can't do anything right.

HARRIS: <u>Whenever we go out, the people always shout, "There goes Jingle Heimer Schmidt!"</u> <u>DA-DA-DADA-DADADA!</u>

PIERCE: Bad, bad vibes. Don't forget the secret methods; mind control, drugs, implants, bad food, bad vibes . . .

JOEY (laughing madly): When I come to the party, I bring all the camels. Seriously, ask me if I'm a truck!

MISS WRIGHT: It's time to take responsibility for our actions. We have to pay for what we've done.

BETH: Why is everyone yelling? Where's my Mommy? I want to go home!

OWEN: It don't matter what we do, it doesn't matter what we say! DON'T YOU GET IT!? WE'RE INSANE!

DANIEL (very softly, not really audible): D . . . is for . . . Daniel.

DR. JANE: What was that? What did you say?

Daniel is trembling now, on the brink or a profound break-through but still unable to say it . . .

DANIEL: I said . . . D is for . . .

DR. JANE: D is for what?

DANIEL: D is for . . .

DR. JANE: I can't hear you.

DANIEL: D is for . . .

The noise is too loud. Daniel is drowned out.

DR. JANE: Enough! All of you, QUIET!

The room is quickly silenced. All the Alters turn and stare at Dr. Jane, stunned.

DR. JANE (addressing all ALTERS): I'm here to help you, but I can't do that if you won't listen. The only way you're getting out of here is if we work together.

Her eyes stay on Daniel.

DR. JANE: Now. You were going to say something. Go ahead.

DANIEL: D is for Daniel. My name is Daniel.

Doctor looks at Daniel, smiles— oddly, her smile is somehow dark, as if she knows a hurtful secret.

DR. JANE (nods): Good to have you back, Daniel.

A sense of strength returns to Daniel's demeanor. He smiles deviously, an evil spark in his eye.

DANIEL (in his OWN VOICE): Thank you, doctor. It's good to be back.

DR. JANE: It's been a long time.

DANIEL: Yes it has.

The Alters stand silently behind Daniel, too afraid to speak.

DR. JANE: Now we can get back to work.

Behind her, the door opens. Dr. Jane and Daniel both look A new DOCTOR (a bearded MAN) enters the room.

We TRACK with Dr. Jane as she walks around the table, behind Daniel, the other Alters around her.

The new Doctor sits down (he does not acknowledge Dr. Jane or the alter personalities). Reviews the file, takes a sip of his coffee, and looks up at Daniel.

DOCTOR: Hello, Daniel. I'm Doctor Blake.
   (beat)
How are we feeling today?

Daniel looks up at him with a strange, self-satisfied smile. Dr. Jane, standing behind him, places a reassuring hand on his shoulder and they SPEAK AT THE SAME TIME:

DANIEL/DR. JANE: I feel fine . . . Doctor.

CUT TO BLACK.

Ideas That Put a New Twist on a Familiar Story

Nothing brings the story home better than a satisfying ending. *The Right Hook* takes a typical story about a guy trying to pick up a girl at a bar and twists it on its head. The title of this short refers to a pick-up line. It also references the way our hero (or anti-hero) ultimately gets the girl when his pick-up lines fail. (He punches her out.)

The short originally ended when Bruno (Dave Scotti) punches the girl in the face. "My mom said, 'If you do a movie like that, every woman in the world is gonna come after you, and you're going to be hated,'" says director Luke Greenfield. "We were terrified, so we did this double ending where the girl is a tough fighter and she says, 'Alright, bitch, you want some of this?' and she kicks Dave's ass. Dave does his line, 'Can I buy you a drink?', she slugs him in the face, and then it ends."

In fact, once the filmmaker found his ending with the guy fully punching this girl in the face as hard as he could, Greenfield went back and based the whole movie around that notion. "We knew that on an autobiographical level. What do you do when you see a hot girl in the bar? What can you possibly say to her? What's your hook?" asks Greenfield. "For the first time, we had this tremendous ending of a guy punching a girl in the face as hard as he could. We went back and developed that as the perfect ending to the movie.

"I was very excited about *The Right Hook*," continues Greenfield. "I knew I had a winner because I knew it starts off in a *Swingers* kind of mode where people are going to yawn and say, 'Here we go again, another *Swingers* rip-off.' I knew it had the unpredictability of shifting tones like Jonathan Demme's *Something Wild*. It starts off with this guy trying to hook up with a girl and it turns into this ultra-violent fight and I wanted it to be so unpredictable. We knew we had a winner just by getting there."

Getting Some Help with Your Ideas

Not all directors can write. Those who can are the true auteurs who can both create and execute their vision. But do not fret if you are one of those directors who has tried unsuccessfully to pen a screenplay. "Frequently I work with directors who don't write," says Jana Sue Memel. "Rarely have I worked with directors without ideas."

Gene Klein's suggestion for directors who do not write: Find a collaborator. "Don't just be a director-for-hire," advises Klein. "Have a distinct point of view, and find somebody who can understand what your point of view of the world is. If they want good execution, they can hire good execution from people who have done it before. But if you have a point of view that really is distinct, that's hard to be duplicated, and you have an advantage over everyone else."

The key to finding a good collaborator is to find someone who understands what your point of view is, what point of view you want to use in your filmmaking, and with whom you can develop a good story. Sometimes directors make a career out of collaborating with one individual. Others collaborate with different writers on each and every project. If you are a nonwriting director who plays well with others, this might be the route for you.

Eduardo Rodriguez is one example of a director with a strong vision who called upon a writer to help him bring his vision to life. Rodriguez was always curious about life after death. "What would happen if you die one day but you don't realize it?" asks Rodriguez. "What if, as you go through the day you start realizing that things are not normal and finally you come to understand that you died?" These nagging questions in the young director's head inspired what ultimately became *Daughter,* the twelve-minute student film that garnered Rodriguez a three-picture deal with Dimension Films.

Rodriguez had always been a huge fan of the horror genre. His goal in crafting *Daughter* was to create an atmosphere where things seemed very wrong. "We don't know exactly why, but things are not always the way we want them to be," says Rodriguez. "Most of my ideas try to say that, and I wanted to create an atmosphere where things are not good."

One way he achieved this result was in his decision to use very little dialogue in the movie. "It was a conscious choice," reveals Rodriguez. "It was the story that dictated not having much dialogue because for most of the movie, it's just a girl on her own finding out what's going on around her, and it was more of an internal journey than an external one that you can easily communicate. The other thing is when you're alone, you don't talk to yourself too much so it would look a little comedic if she's like 'Oh my God, what's going on here?' "

Daughter was a school project, so Rodriguez had an entire semester to write the script. "I had the idea before we went to development," admits Rodriguez. "But we had probably three months to write it."

In actuality, the first draft was written in a week. It came out to about fifteen pages. At the time Rodriguez was the sole writer. Knowing he needed a tighter screenplay, Rodriguez enlisted the help of his classmate, Sean Garmen, and the two started rewriting. They worked together closely to tighten the story and cut down the length of the script. The final script was twelve pages. The final running time of the short was about fourteen minutes.

AMAZING STORIES

No matter what format you select, what genre you choose, or where you get the idea for your film, one constant remains in filmmaking—it all comes down to telling a great story. Speaking of which, here's a doozy.

When Luke Greenfield was a boy, he was obsessed with Steven Spielberg. Growing up in Connecticut, the family had no connections to Hollywood. But that did not stop Greenfield's mom. "She was worried about me wanting to become a director and how impossible that is," says Greenfield. "She wanted me to become a doctor or a lawyer. So she wrote Steven Spielberg this very passionate letter telling him she was worried and asking this guy if I had what it took to make it."

Included with the letter was a research paper Greenfield had written in high school years before Spielberg had won any Academy Awards called "Steven Spielberg: The Star They Wouldn't Let Shine," because he had been snubbed for his earlier work. Somehow Spielberg saw Greenfield's films, read his mom's letter, and read his research paper, and he wanted to contact the aspiring filmmaker. He told his assistant to find Greenfield. All they had was the research paper which was marked "Luke Greenfield, Staples High School." "They had to find out where I was, and they called the high school," recalls Greenfield. "'This is Steven Spielberg's office. We need Luke's address.' My school hung up on them."

Finally, a letter came addressed to Greenfield. "Steven had written this two-page handwritten letter to me, which took me years to really understand what he was saying," shares Greenfield. "He gave me the best advice ever—*tell a great story, but the 'truth' in the telling is what reaches* audiences *everywhere.* If you look at all the great Spielberg films, they all have amazing stories. The real essence of these films is that he's talking about themes and characters that we all can relate to."

Whether your idea is completely original, based on a piece of underlying material, inspired by a true-life event, or derived from an alternative source, remember that it is the foundation of your short film. You might have great style and excellent presentation, but if the story is not solid, these other elements will not bring you to the next level on their own accord. Once you focus in on an idea, be sure it strikes a chord with you and your audience. Great ideas make memorable films. Memorable films launch careers.

3

Budget:
How to Spend the Money

"On a short film, the budget is the biggest challenge. That problem doesn't necessarily go away the higher up you get. There are always those battles. You're trying to do more than you can with a limited amount of resources, and if you're not, I think you're almost doing something wrong because you're not pushing it far enough."

—Gary Bryman, producer

DISCOUNT FILMMAKING

In all filmmaking—short films and features—it's important to set and stay within a budget to be sure the film sees the light of day. Luke Greenfield wrote a screenplay titled *Echo Lake* with the help of his two friends, David Scotti and Dean Marsico. Mirroring the strategy implemented by Ben Affleck and Matt Damon with *Good Will Hunting*, the plan was for Greenfield to direct the film and his two friends to star in it. But the trio kept hitting roadblocks, and they were unable to get the project off the ground.

Part of the problem lay in raising the money to produce the movie. They truly thought they could raise the funds because they had just seen Kevin Smith do that with *Clerks*. Scotti's parents lived in a very wealthy town in New Jersey, not too far from Redbank, where Smith grew up. And although the group was unable to raise enough money to make a feature, they were able to assemble some capital. In fact, they managed to collect $28,000 from local residents and friends of the family.

"We had a whole package we had slaved on," explains Greenfield. The presentation included a script, biographies on the filmmakers and cast, a budget, a schedule, and a business plan outlining how investors would make their money back. Scotti's brother was an attorney, and he helped the young men piece the package together.

"If we made this film, we promised them the world," says Greenfield. "We didn't care about money. I still don't care about money. It was all about making your movie and proving to the world that you're a great filmmaker. Dave wanted to prove that he was a great actor."

But $28,000 was not enough to produce *Echo Lake*. "So we had this money and we didn't know what to do," says Greenfield. "There was one scene in *Echo Lake* where one of the main characters gets beat up by a lesbian in a bar. I was talking to [fellow filmmaker] Trevor Sands about ideas for a short film. And Trevor thought that sounded funny."

Greenfield and Scotti worked together to adapt that scene into a stand-alone short film script they eventually called *The Right Hook* (see *Chapter Two: Concept*). Once the script was complete, they forged ahead. In fact, they raced into production.

The film was shot in four days, but they ran out of money as soon as they wrapped. "It was so poorly planned out that by the time we finished shooting, we had no money to develop the film," says Greenfield. "We had no money to do anything. This is the horror of making a movie."

On the verge of desperation, Greenfield had no choice but to become resourceful. He went to every person in the business he had ever worked for and asked them to help. One of his mentors was Hal Harrison, who ran post-production at Paramount Television. "I begged him and said we had shot this footage. The negative was at 4MC, and they wouldn't let it go because we owed them money."

Greenfield's producer borrowed money from her sister so they could develop the film. Hal Harrison helped get them a deal to telecine (color time) the negative straight to video so at the very least they could see what they had shot. "We didn't see this footage for months," says Greenfield. "We had shot it in October, and we didn't see it until Christmastime."

In planning the shoot, they were able to purchase most of what they needed at a discount, or in some instances, get it donated for free. "Panavision gave us two cameras for free," says Greenfield. "Kodak gave us a good deal on some film. We had a DP [director of photography] who worked for next to nothing. You have to pay the crew and craft service. We had the stunt team from *Fight Club*, this guy Noon Orsatti and his team, onboard. He loved the script so much that they did all the stunts for free."

So how was the $28,000 spent? That seems like sufficient money to produce a short film. A lot of the money was actually spent on film stock, on the crew, on food, on the equipment, and on developing the negative. But the big costs of the short film came later in editing and telecine.

One of the most important meetings Harrison helped Greenfield set up was with Cyril Drabinsky, president of Deluxe Labs. "He just looked at me and asked 'Why should I ever develop your film for free and print your negative?'" recalls Greenfield. "I looked him in the eye and said, 'Because one day I'm gonna get a studio feature film off this and I'll come to you.'" Drabinsky admired Greenfield's conviction and gave him everything he needed to complete the film for free.

Cyril Drabinsky and Hal Harrison also talked other people into helping out the young filmmakers. Pac Title did all the titles, dissolves, and opticals for free. Even Todd AO was willing to work with the filmmakers and negotiate a good price for their services.

Making films can be an expensive endeavor. Full-length features average around $20 million a piece. And although some low-budget, independent films like *Swingers* are shot for under a million dollars, other special-effects extravaganzas such as *Spiderman* can reach beyond the $100 million range. Though the stakes (and the costs) in short filmmaking aren't usually that high, these films can also be quite expensive. This next section will show how you can keep costs down while getting the most value for the money you spend.

FROM ZERO TO FIFTY GRAND

The truth is, you can make a short for any price. "You can spend no money on a short and do it well if it's the right concept and you have the right elements come together," says producer Gary Bryman.

Peter Lord made one of his first shorts for close to nothing. *Adam* was an animated film about the planet's first man learning the ways of the world. "*Adam* is an interesting case because that was done with no budget," says Lord. "It cost money, of course, but nobody paid for it. Those were the dear happy days when there was so much money in the company, I just took three months off, had a quiet corner in the studio, didn't disturb anybody, and quietly made the film. We were making commercials at the same time. We owned the cameras. We owned the equipment. We just did it without any budget at all."

Owning your own equipment will always help bring down your budget. So will old-fashioned skills like borrowing and bartering. The thing to remember at the end of the day is not to let your budgetary constraints affect the overall quality of your product. "You can spend a million dollars or ten dollars," says producer Steve Hein. "Studios don't care as long as it meets their expectations of what it should look like."

And what should a short look like? It should look as professional as it can. If possible, it should look like any other film that studio executives would screen. That might imply shooting on 35mm film stock, which is clearly more expensive than other formats.

"Do not do it half-assed," suggests Hein. "This is something that you only want to do once. You're going to be investing so much time and so much money in it that you want to get it right the first time. Better to be twenty thousand dollars in debt and have a great film, than be ten thousand dollars in debt and have it look like shit. Give it one hundred percent, and give it everything you have until there's nothing left to give because that's the only way you're going to end up with the best product."

Here is a look at what several short films cost to make. Remember, in most cases, the actual cost would be much higher if the filmmakers had been unable to call in favors and get products and services donated for free or below cost.

Adam	0
Battle of the Sexes	$10,000
Daughter	$18,000
Truly Committed	$20,000
George Lucas in Love	$25,000
The Right Hook	$28,000
Peep Show	$30,000
Ray's Male Heterosexual Dance Hall	$35,000
Inside	$40,000
Say Virgil	$125,000

Let's say you are able to raise a lot of money. That does not necessarily mean that you should start thinking about making a feature-length film instead of a short. It's more important to get the highest-quality film you can from the resources you have at hand. "I think it [would be] better to make a seven-minute movie, because you're going to have a *fantastic*-looking seven-minute movie," says Hein. "It's going to be an amazing short that everyone's going to love as opposed to a stressed-out, under-budget, over-worked, shot-under-schedule feature film that no one's gonna watch."

Why not stack the odds in your favor and take your best shot? "You need to do whatever it's going to take to execute your film properly," says Hein. "More than likely you're going to be spending a lot of your own money, so I think if you're going to do it right, you want to do it right once and you don't want to have to do it again."

THE BEG AND BARTER SYSTEM

Okay, so you don't have $50,000 in the bank. You do still have lots of options for financing your film. Sometimes vendors are willing to cut deals with young filmmakers, but it might take some effort convincing them why they should gamble on you. And because you are not offering them large sums of money, you need to appeal to their sensitive side. "My mom always taught me to write a passionate letter," says Luke Greenfield, who still uses the technique today, especially when trying to convince a major star to act in a feature he is directing. "For me, it's always about getting the person in the room and opening up your heart and telling them everything you feel, and why you'll die if you don't make this movie, and why they have to help."

Establish Your Credibility

Establishing credibility is key to being taken seriously in Hollywood. "The Steven Spielberg support really helped a lot. People took that as legitimacy," admits Greenfield, referring to the letter the *Jurassic* director had written him years before. "I had made this student film at USC that showed that I could at least make a movie and that I knew what I was doing."

When push comes to shove, you just have to take a chance and ask. The worst that can happen is they say "No." "I was literally just begging, 'You have to take a shot on me,'" says Greenfield.

"The trick is, if you don't have the resources and you don't have the money, how do you beg, borrow, and steal and transform your passion in the project to have that become your currency?" asks producer Gary Bryman. "When you're starting out, that's really all you have—an unlimited level of passion. And you're gonna need it."

You must be persistent. "You fax them letters and then they say they don't get the letters," says Greenfield. "You mail them letters and then you make sure they get the letters. Then you start calling like crazy. And you don't stop until you get a five-minute meeting. We used to joke about *Wall Street* where Bud Fox (Charlie Sheen) would go to Gordon Gekko (Michael Douglas) and say, 'Life comes down to a few key moments, and this could be one of them.' And that's what it is. You have one minute to sink or swim."

Show Your Passion

Greenfield remembers walking into Cyril Drabinsky's office, the president of Deluxe Labs, quite clearly. "We had two minutes to convince him to do this," says Greenfield. "He heard us out, and we could tell he was seeing if we were passionate. It's not much to him. It's a ten-minute short film. We're not talking about a lot of film stock or a lot of cost to him. It may be annoying for him, but he did it. It's about showing them your passion and not taking no."

Still, Greenfield had one ace in the hole. He had already shot the movie, so Greenfield had actual footage to show to vendors. "I had a rough cut of *The Right Hook* on video, so I went in and sold Drabinsky with the rough cut, and I made him laugh," says Greenfield. "That was the kicker. We got him to laugh. I had something to show. Here's our product, please help us finish it."

The fact that Greenfield's short was successful in launching his feature career as a director certainly reaffirmed Drabinsky's decision to help the aspiring filmmaker. It probably also helped that Greenfield was true to his word and used Deluxe Labs on his first two studio features, *The Animal* and *The Girl Next Door*. All this might be why Drabinsky was willing to take a gamble on another aspiring filmmaker when Trevor Sands approached him the next year with a similar proposition.

"I got a big break at a prominent lab that offered me free processing and prints essentially because a friend of mine, the year before, had gotten the same deal with them and landed a big feature and had come back to them with his feature," says Sands. "So it had paid off. My friend, Luke Greenfield, who had done *The Right Hook,* called the head of the lab and said, 'Trevor is a great guy, and if you're ever gonna give someone else a free package, he's the guy to do it.' I knew Luke from USC, and it's another great example of how those relationships really have value."

Make and Maintain Contacts

Of course, if you do not have someone to make a call for you, the next best thing is to start building those relationships yourself. Eric Kripke worked many odd jobs in the movie business, making contacts with many people who would eventually aid him in the future. "The best way to get stuff for free is to start making contacts. And the best way to start making contacts is to get into production," advises Kripke. "Get onto as many sets as humanly possible. Sneak your way on if you have to. And then start shaking hands and meeting people. Get into it. Get your hands dirty. Be annoying. Collect cards and follow up on those cards. Call people."

One last piece of advice: "Work your ass off," says Kripke. "I recommend being a PA [production assistant]. If you're a PA, never walk. Run. Bust your ass. Show them how badly you want this, and they'll remember you and help you when you need help."

CHOOSE WHERE TO SPEND YOUR MONEY

The next component of budget filmmaking is, of course, to get the most bang for your buck. Take the money you do have and make it count.

Joe Nussbaum thought he could shoot *George Lucas in Love* for around $10,000, but that figure turned out to be a pipe dream. In actuality, he wound up spending close to $25,000 on the film. His mission was to make each penny count. "We had a real directive to put all the money on the screen, so we actually spent a lot of money on things that people don't usually spend money on," says Nussbaum.

For instance, the production design team actually built a dorm room set so they did not have to shoot in an actual cramped dorm room. By building the set on a sound stage, it was a lot easier to move around and set up interesting shots. This was something cinematographer Eric Haase really pushed for because it allowed for the ability to do more with the camera because of the freedom of movement. They also managed to transform what could have potentially been another rather boring dorm room into something that looked really cool.

A lot of the money was also spent on the film to video transfer. "We got a really nice telecine, and that cost a lot," says Nussbaum. "But again, it was worth it because it was on the screen. We shot on 35mm. We spent a lot of money on music, on the score. We had a live orchestra with thirteen players. It was just upping the ante of production value. We still crimped and saved on everything as much as we could, but I think we knew what we wanted to spend money on and what we didn't want to spend money on."

CHOOSE WHERE *NOT* TO SPEND YOUR MONEY

So what did the *George Lucas in Love* budget *not* spend money on? "We didn't pay anyone," admits Nussbaum. "We tried to not pay as many people as we possibly could. We certainly didn't pay the actors." However, the actors did end up receiving deferred payment once the short earned a profit.

A lot of the crew were also working for free. "We got a free camera package from Panavision that was amazing," says Nussbaum, who credits that gift to cinematographer Eric Haase and producer Joseph Levy. "The planets aligned, and somehow it happened."

All the post-production was done at the trailer company where Nussbaum worked. "I'm sure they figured, 'So one of our guys is doing some side project. It's not gonna go anywhere,'" says Nussbaum. "I wasn't the first person to do a side project there. That happens all over town all the time. There probably isn't a post house in this city where tonight, some editor isn't going in at eleven o'clock to cut his friend's short film. That's totally the norm. It happens everywhere."

DON'T FORGET POST-PRODUCTION

The most common mistake filmmakers make is not allotting sufficient funds to complete post-production. "A lot of times people have twenty grand to get the film in the can and they think they can finish post for a thousand dollars," says Steve Hein. "If you spend twenty thousand dollars on production, there's a chance you'll be spending ten to fifteen thousand dollars on post. A lot of times people shoot movies and then the film will sit on a shelf for two years while they try to figure out how to finish them."

Eric Kripke agrees. "Giving yourself enough money for post-production is something that almost no one does successfully. When we cut *Truly Committed,* we were still students so we could use USC's Avids. *Truly Committed* took a long time to cut only because we were doing it in between classes.

"*Battle of the Sexes* was just about making friends with people in the industry," continues Kripke. "The guy who cut it was working at a company that cut infomercials, so we would get on his machine during his off-hours. He'd get out by seven at night and he'd cut until two in the morning. He was the editor, and he was using his own Avid equipment. You just rent out the drive space."

SHOW ME THE MONEY

There is no secret to raising money for short films. Do it any way you can. "Typically these things are director-financed, so it's about finding the money," says Steve Hein. "If you don't happen to have twenty to thirty thousand dollars laying around in your back pocket all the time, there's credit cards, family, friends, etc. There's also a variety of grants out there, and corporate sponsorship is also becoming quite popular."

Eric Kripke cashed in some savings bonds to finance his first film, but he still needed more cash. "Gary, Steve, and I went to a bank to take out a loan to supposedly pay for college tuition, and we just put the money right into the movie," reveals Kripke. "For all you kids out there, banks don't ask how you spend the money. At least they don't care as long as you pay them back. But you must pay them back."

Trevor Sands worked hard for the money and just saved up until he could afford to go into production. "I did three studio jobs and as a writer in the WGA [Writers Guild of America] with a decent rate, I had that money," says Sands. "So that I didn't spend all my cash, I used some credit cards, and I took out a twenty-thousand-dollar loan for the specific purpose of the film, which I very quickly paid back. But it was all a tax write-off."

Sands was lucky. If he had not been working as a writer and making the kind of money writers make, it would have taken him much longer to save up to make his short. "That's the big problem with filmmaking in general—it's expensive," says Sands. "Even back in the day when I was shooting spec commercials, just to get a crew out there and shoot a couple shots, it costs thousands of dollars, and there's really no way around that."

SHORT BUDGETS REVEALED

What follows are budgets for actual short films. Here you can see how the money was allocated. In many instances, you might notice that no funds were allocated to some of the major categories. This is most likely due to the fact that these goods or services were donated to the production. Trevor Sands spent $40,000 on *Inside*. "The actual dollar value of what's on the screen, if I had to pay full rate for everything, is probably one hundred fifty to two hundred thousand dollars," reveals Sands.

By perusing Sand's budget on the following pages, you can see where he spent money and where he saved money. You can also see a comparison of the estimated budget and what they actually spent on the shoot. He did pay his crew, but he only paid them $50 per day, which clearly kept costs down, as many crew members typically earn more than $50 per hour. He did not pay the cast at all. Using a SAG experimental agreement, the actors will receive deferred pay only if the film makes money. Knowing that a well-fed cast and crew is a happy cast and crew, Sands spent almost $2,500 on food for the three-day shoot. Another huge savings was that most of his post-production costs were donated for free. This saved the filmmaker a great deal of money.

You can compare Sand's budget with Eduardo Rodriguez's budget for *Daughter,* which follows. Most of Rodriguez's labor costs were eliminated because his fellow Florida State students worked for free as part of their academic requirements. Similarly, the school owned most of the necessary equipment, so Rodriguez saved a good deal of money not having to pay rental fees. Much of Rodriguez's budget was spent in post-production. Unlike Sands, he did not have a lab to donate their services.

As you compare and contrast these budgets, think about where you might be able to call in favors and save money. Similarly, what aspects of production will be most important for you to spend money on? To help make some of these decisions, it is best to know the least amount of crew and equipment you will need. The next few chapters will help you make an informed decision.

Quality Filmed Entertainment
INSIDE

Bid date: 5/14/01

Production Co.:	**Quality Filmed Entertainment**
Address:	5478 WILSHIRE BLVD
	LOS ANGELES CA
Telephone:	323.939.7274
Fax:	323.939.6836
Job #:	
Contract:	Steve Hein/Gary Bryman
Director:	Trevor Sands
Producer:	Gary Bryman, Steve Hein
DP:	Eric Haase
Art Director:	Paul Macherey
Editor:	Trevor Sands
Pre-Production Days:	7
Build & Strike Days:	3 Hours: 12
Pre-Light Days:	Hours: 12
Studio Shoot Days:	2 Hours: 14
Location Days:	1 Hours: 12
Location(s):	Padded Cell

SUMMARY OF ESTIMATED PRODUCTION COSTS		ESTIMATED	ACTUAL	VARIANCE
1 Pre-production & Wrap Costs	Totals A & C	3,367	1,384.69	(1,982.31)
2 Shooting Labor	Total B	4,849	7,778.00	2,929.00
3 Location & Travel Expenses	Total D	3,930	4,098.70	168.70
4 Props, Wardrobe & Animals	Total E	560	358.00	(202.00)
5 Studio & Set Construction Costs	Total F, G & H	3,500	6,130.15	2,630.15
6 Equipment Costs	Total I	6,520	8,873.90	2,353.90
7 Filmstock, Process & Print	Total J	5,400	8,501.18	3,101.18
8 Miscellaneous	Total K	500	1,700.00	1,200.00
9	**Sub-total A to K**	28,626	38,824.62	10,198.62
10 Director /Creative Fees (not included in Direct Costs)	Total L			
11 Insurance				
12	**Sub-total Direct Costs**	28,626	38,824.62	10,198.62
13 Production Fee				
14 Talent Labor & expenses	Totals M & N			
15 Editorial & Finishing	Totals O & P	2,000	4,349.50	2,349.50
16				
17 Other				
18 Other				
19				

Contracted Total	30,626	**GRAND TOTAL**	**$30, 626**	**$43,174.12**	**$12,548.12**
Contingency Day					

COMMENTS
1 Prep Day
3 12 Hour Days
1 Wrap day

"Daughter" 35mm Thesis Budget
2001

Running Time: 10 mins.   Shooting Ratio: 10:1
Shooting Days: 9   New Stock?   Yes

Includes Variable Pricing   Cutting Ratio: 3:1
Meets MINIMUM Delivery Reqs.

Prepared By: N. Senger

Acct#	Category Title	Page	Total
1000	CAST/DAY PLAYERS/EXTRAS	1	$0
	Total Above-The-Line		**$0**
1500	FILM/SOUND STOCK	1	$2,384
2000	PRODUCTION LABORATORY/TRANSFER	1	$3,356
2500	EQUIPMENT RENTAL	1	$430
3000	PRODUCTION DESIGN	2	$1,863
3500	SET MANAGEMENT	2	$63
4000	OFFICE MANAGEMENT	2	$379
9999	OVER PRODUCTION BUDGET	2	$486
4500	CATERING AND CRAFT SERVICES	3	$1,821
	Total Production		**$10,782**
5000	EDITING EQUIPMENT/EXPENDABLES	3	$81
5500	POST LABORATORY/TRANSFER	3	$3,325
6000	NEGATIVE CUTTING	3	$2,239
6500	TITLES	4	$468
7000	VISUAL AND OPTICAL EFFECTS	4	$144
7500	MUSIC/SCORING	4	$13
8000	PUBLICITY/FESTIVAL	4	$171
8500	OTHER POST-PRODUCTION COSTS	4	$200
	Total Post-Production		**$6,641**
	10% Contingency		$1,742
	TOTAL ABOVE-THE-LINE		**$0**
	TOTAL BELOW-THE-LINE		**$17,423**
	TOTAL ABOVE & BELOW-THE-LINE		**$17,423**
	GRAND TOTAL		**$19,165**

"I just didn't want to shoot something on DV. I felt like I wanted to present something that in eight minutes looked as good as any feature film you'd see in the market."

—Trevor Sands, writer/director

HOW REAL MOVIES ARE MADE

During pre-production on *George Lucas in Love,* Joe Nussbaum called cinematographer Eric Haase to give him some bad news. He told the director of photography that due to budgetary restrictions, they would have to shoot the movie on 16mm film instead of 35mm as they had hoped. "I vividly remember driving in my car having this conversation," says Haase. "I told him, 'I know what I can do with this, and I know what you can do with this. I think if you're going to put this much money into it, let's put the little bit more that it's going to take to shoot on 35mm. This is how real movies are made. Let's make a real movie.'"

Haase makes a lot of sense. With a short, you will not save hundreds of thousands of dollars by shooting on 16mm over 35mm. "You're not going to shoot that much film stock on a short, so that's not a big part of the budget," explains Haase.

In addition, you might be able to call in some favors to get a deal on certain equipment that in the long run makes it more economical to shoot on a more expensive format. "Maybe I know this guy at Panavision who can hook us up with a camera rental on 35mm and make it comparable to what you would pay for a 16mm package," says Haase. In either case, the lighting units are basically going to be the same, so changing formats has little to no economic impact there, either.

Nussbaum weighed his decision carefully before calling Haase back to let him know that they would indeed shoot on 35mm. "And we knew," says Haase. "When we saw the dailies and when we were doing the telecine, Joe said 'I think this is going to be really good. I'm so glad we shot on 35mm.'"

WELL EQUIPPED

In this chapter, we will explore some of your major equipment needs. This discussion is not all encompassing, and there will be additional tools that are necessary for you to make your short. This is simply an introduction to some of the big-ticket items you will need to consider when planning for your film such as camera, lighting equipment, audio equipment, and editing system.

Because filmmaking takes place on location all over the world, most major cities have rental houses where you can rent equipment to shoot a movie. Always remember to plan in advance so you can reserve equipment for the dates you will need it. Most houses require proof of insurance because the equipment is so expensive. These vendors generally provide that insurance to customers for a fee, or they will refer you to a company that offers policies to cover your shoot.

Plan your shoot to maximize use of the equipment. Many houses charge a one-day rate for the entire weekend because they are generally closed on Sundays. Weekly rates tend to be slightly better than daily rates. Students should always ask if student discounts are available because you might be able to save a lot of money this way.

If you are having trouble finding what you need, call your local film commission. There is usually one in every state and every major city in the country. There are also film offices in major cities abroad. You can also try logging onto the Internet to find vendors who rent filmmaking equipment.

"I don't think there's ever been a better time to be a short filmmaker with the resources and technology where it is," says Gary Bryman. "With digital cameras coming down in price and Final Cut Pro 3 being introduced, there really are tools at a filmmaker's disposal to tell the story they want to tell. The only thing that's holding them back is their imagination."

"It always starts with having a good idea and a good script," says producer Steve Hein. "I think it's best if somebody takes some time working in some aspect of the entertainment industry to get access to the resources to make the best film possible. That may be through borrowed equipment or just through advice, because it's often rare that things happen in a bubble. At least put a year or two in to get the lay of the land, and build relationships so you can get that free camera when you need it."

VISUAL FORMATS

One of the first considerations filmmakers have is whether to shoot on film or video. Once they make that decision, they must determine which format of film or video would be best to use. The next two sections will outline the major options and explore the pros and cons of each format.

Video

The following chart lists the various video formats in ascending order of quality.

Video

Fisher Price PXL2000 . . . . Lowest Quality

VHS

Hi-8

Mini-DV

Beta SP

Digi-Beta

High Definition . . . . Highest Quality

The **Fisher Price PXL2000** is a 2,000-pixel camera that records onto an audio tape in black and white. You get three minutes per tape, and you can flip over the tape to record on both sides. "That's pretty much the bottom of the barrel," says Haase, whose very first camera was, in fact, a PXL2000. "You can't get those anymore, but they do sell them on eBay. Usually that kind of footage pops up in a music video."

VHS camcorders are analog devices. They are not really used much anymore since the price for digital video has come down. "I used to make 8mm video or VHS camcorder and cut it VCR to VCR in a linear fashion to edit it," says Haase. "But digital video has opened it up to everybody. With mini-DV [digital video] you can put it in your computer and edit it in a nonlinear way, move it around and really experiment with it, and it's pretty cheap to do."

Hi-8 is a small tape video format that is superior to VHS but inferior to DV/mini-DV. The image quality and resolution are better on Hi-8 than VHS, and the tapes and camera are smaller in size. Hi-8 was the main format of consumer camcorders before mini-DV came along, and you can still buy some really cheap Hi-8 camcorders. The biggest downside is that the tape format is analog, and image quality is lost in doing any editing or dubbing. Hi-8 has always been a mostly consumer format.

"The quality of mini-DV is significantly better than Hi-8 used to be, but in the relative sense of those low-end video formats," says Haase. "But in the broad sense, it's not that much of a huge step regarding quality of image."

DV and **mini-DV** are the same thing—they are just physically different tape sizes for cameras and playback machines. The advantage of DV or mini-DV is that these formats are very accessible to so many people. The technology is small and portable. Most people know how to use them fairly well even if they do not know all the features of the camera. You can move the camera easily. You do not generally need permits to shoot because it can be inconspicuous. It is digital, so when you are editing, there is not that much loss in quality. The disadvantage is that it does not look as great as film. Sometimes it is not taken as seriously in the professional arena.

"We're used to seeing soap operas, games shows, and TV news on video," says Haase. "And we're used to seeing dramatic content that we buy into as fiction on film. Subconsciously, psychologically, that plays into it a great deal. When you're trying to sell a fictional story on a thirty-frame format like mini-DV, I think that plays a big part where you're like this is just [like] a soap opera and it seems somewhat cheesier."

Most of the camcorders you can purchase today at electronics stores like Best Buy are mini-DV. You can shoot on it, and the quality will be okay. Plug the player into your computer, and you can do some nonlinear editing. Finally, you can put it back out to tape with no loss in quality. Add titles. Add effects in After Effects. Whatever you want to do is totally accessible.

Beta SP and **Digi-Beta** are professional-quality tape formats. They are mostly used for post-production activities, although they are also sometimes used for image acquisition as well. This format offers high signal to noise, low headwear, reduced dropouts, and outstanding durability.

There is also a big difference between DV and high-definition. A consumer DV camera runs at thirty frames per second. High-definition runs at twenty-four frames per second. "DV is kind of the bottom of the barrel as far as the quality of the video image," says Haase. "Above that you have Beta SP, digi-Beta, and then high definition, which has even more resolution as a format than any of those."

The advantage of **high definition** is that the resolution is so high. If you ultimately want to output it to film later on, it will hold up pretty well.

You can shoot on high definition cheaply—you do not have to pay for the film stock or the processing, and you can output it to film for exhibition. Soon there will be digital distribution and we will have the ability to watch films digitally. In fact, we will be able to acquire the picture, distribute film, *and* exhibit it digitally on the high-definition format. That is a huge cost savings as far as film stock, processing, printing, and for distribution.

The other advantage of high definition or shooting a video is that you have a monitor on the set. "What you see is what you get," says Haase. "So when you're lighting, if you want to tweak this, you tweak it. If you want it to be a little more yellow or a little more blue, you can see it right there. And it's already in the digital world, so if you want to do digital effects or digital color correction, there's no expensive scanning process when you have to scan the film to do the digital effects that way. Doing it in the digital world is a bonus."

Film

The following chart lists the various film formats in ascending order of quality.

Film
8mm . . . . Lowest Quality
16mm
35mm
Imax . . . . Highest Quality

8mm, or **Super 8,** is what everybody shot their home movies on in the 1960s and 1970s. Essentially the same things, 8mm has perforations on both sides of the film, whereas Super 8 has perforations only on one side. Either way, it is low-quality, very low-resolution film. The color reproduction is not very good. "A lot of times now it's just used for flashbacks or dream sequences," says Haase. "It gets really grainy if you blow it up to 35mm."

16mm is used for a lot of student films. The exposure for 16mm is the same as the exposure for 35mm. Therefore, the lighting principles are the same. A lot of television shows like *Scrubs, Malcolm in the Middle,* and *Roswell* are shot on 16mm. 16mm cameras are smaller, more portable, and a little more flexible. Loading the magazine takes less time and less skill to do. If you are doing a lot of handheld work, running around, or Steadicam shots with a Stedicam guy who is not so experienced, the 16mm camera is light and easier to work with. For those reasons and for the cost savings, 16mm is a format that you might choose.

However, there are some costs to consider with 16mm film—film processing costs, telecine costs, etc. It is still less expensive than 35mm because you are using about half as much film, so there is half as much cost on the stock, processing, etc. If you are doing a theatrical feature and you have to blow it up later, keep in mind that it gets more grainy and has less resolution. *Leaving Las Vegas* was shot in 16mm and then blown up to 35mm.

Technically, a **35mm** camera is a little more difficult to use for a camera assistant than 16mm. The focus is more critical, so you have to have a better focus puller. You might get film that is out of focus if you have inexperienced people using it. Another downside is that the equipment is larger and, therefore, more difficult to handle, there is more of it, and you need bigger trucks to carry it.

That said, most professional filmmakers agree that 35mm is the standard for high-quality feature and short films. "I think 35mm is still the best way to acquire images for motion pictures," says Haase. "If you want to go to high definition, you have the ability to go there. You can bump it down to any other format, or you can print it and project it. You can blow it up to 70mm IMAX and it will hold up decently well, although that's not a very common application. The disadvantages are obviously cost, equipment, etc."

"35mm is a bitch to develop, meaning it's expensive," says filmmaker Eric Kripke. "At the end of the day, short filmmaking is all about cost efficiency, trying to spend as little money as possible. What's most important, however, is that it looks like film. If you're gonna spend all the money it takes to do a short, my feeling was, even when I did *Truly Committed,* that

I wanted to shoot 1:185. I wanted to make movies. I wanted to shoot in that ratio. I wanted experience as to how to frame and compose with these dimensions. So I would say whether you shoot in video or film, you want it to look as real and professional as possible."

FILM VERSUS VIDEO

The main reason Joe Nussbaum spent so much money on production design, why he shot *George Lucas in Love* on 35mm, and why he spent so much money on the transfer is because Hollywood executives expect the finished product to look a certain way. "One of the things I had learned in development and Joseph [Levy] had learned in the agencies, is in this business people are unable to look beyond the core presentation," says Nussbaum. "That's why I think student films aren't always showable because you're judged on everything. Things that you shouldn't be judged on, you're judged on. That's the nature of the beast. It's a competitive industry. It's unfair.

"It would be nice to judge a great story told with great acting shot on a VHS camcorder," continues Nussbaum. "But that's not the nature of the business. You've got to have great presentation. That's the first barrier. If you have a beautiful looking image, then they'll see if the acting is good. Then they'll look and see if the storytelling is good. But first it has to be beautiful."

There are movies that break the rules like *Clerks* and *The Blair Witch Project,* where people are able to see beyond the actual presentation. But in a short where you are trying to show the major players that you can play in their league, it is harder to do so. Studio execs want to know if new filmmakers can play at their level. "My advice would be, cut your teeth on cheaper stuff," says Nussbaum. "Don't allow yourself to live in a vacuum. Show people your work. Get feedback from honest people you trust. Don't surround yourself with people who are just gonna say, 'You're brilliant.' Surround yourself with people who are gonna challenge you and try to make your work better.

"That's what is so great about film school," says Nussbaum. "It's very easy when you're making a short film to take someone's criticism and blow it off and say, 'They don't get my work. They don't understand me.' I think a lot of times that's just lying to yourself, and people should get an honest evaluation of what they can do."

Steve Hein agrees. "Anything that distracts them from the quality of the picture oftentimes gives them a reason to pass. That's why we've always been big proponents of making sure things were shot on 35mm. In the last year, we've put a footnote in that. I've seen some stuff on 24P [24 frames per second progressive], which is pretty amazing, so I think that ultimately it's really about the content. If you can shoot stuff on 24P, or shoot stuff on DV and give it a cinema look, as long as it's still funny, or still scary . . . you don't want to be distracting and you want to make sure it shows great production value.

"24P is finally there, depending on what you're shooting it for," continues Hein. "If it's something that's very story- and content-driven, it's not something that necessarily has to look ravishing and beautiful, but if it's trying to make somebody laugh, that's reasonable to shoot in 24P. But if you want something that's lavish and beautiful and crazy, you'll want to shoot on 35mm because people you're competing with and people who are watching and judging you are conditioned for 35mm."

You can transfer the film to a tape, but that can be an expensive process. You adjust the color while you are doing that in telecine. You string it up and transfer to video tape either the whole roll or certain takes you want, and you can transfer to DV cam or mini-DV tape and put that in your computer and edit it.

If the film is only ever going to be shown on video, like for broadcast, you can leave it on tape and work with it on tape. "A TV show I shot for Paramount was shot on 35mm, then transferred to digi-Beta," says Haase. "Digi-Beta as a format is better than DV cam or mini-DV, but you could use mini-DV or DV cam if you want and air it. It's not going to look as good as the digi-Beta format. Do all the editing on a nonlinear system digi-Beta, full video resolution; assemble the final show; and that's it. It never goes past that.

You can cut on those systems and still conform the negative to that edit. Then you make prints of that negative, which you send out to theaters."

"I've seen some great-looking movies that sucked," says Gary Bryman. "If your material and the story you're trying to tell can transcend medium, which oftentimes it can, at the end of the day you just have to do everything in your power to get that story told with whatever you have access to."

BARGAIN-BASEMENT PRICES

As you know from reading the previous chapter on budgets, it is possible to get equipment for your shoot at a discounted rate or for free. Until you start making calls to price out various equipment packages, keep an open mind. You might find some bargains because it is a slow week, or perhaps your passion inspired a vendor to work with you at a price you can afford.

"When you make movies, you're always begging, borrowing, and stealing," notes Steve Hein, who says that the equipment you decide to use really depends on what you can find and what you can get for free. "Your project could be shooting in 35mm, and it could be cheaper than shooting in 24P just because you're able to get a free camera, free processing, and free film, but you had to rent the 24P camera."

"You almost always have to pay for processing," says Eric Haase. "It's hard to get processing for free, although sometimes you can get film stock donated."

If you do shoot on a rougher medium, be sure to employ those things and be aware of them. "Don't try to shoot something that looks like a huge, big movie with only twenty-five bucks and a camcorder," says Hein. "Use that to your advantage somehow."

"Make pie if you have those resources," says Gary Bryman. "Don't try to make pie with cake ingredients. Try to use the medium to use your limited resources to your advantage. Don't try and make it look amazing. It's never going to look that way."

Hein and Bryman did exactly this when shooting *Terry Tate: Office*

Linebacker on DV. This was shot for less than $5,000, just like those NFL sports videos that are really rough and handheld. They were able to really use the medium to their advantage. "The short was originally shot over a weekend, just real rough, thrown together with a DV camera in an office building," says Hein. "The concept was a linebacker who worked in an office enforcing office policy. So basically if you didn't put coffee in the coffee machine, or if you left photocopies in the photocopier, he would come and take you down linebacker style."

The short was written and directed by newcomer Rawson Thurber. The short went on to catch the attention of Reebok, and it became the company's NFL ad campaign for the following football season. "They gave us a budget to shoot four short films, four commercials, eight stadium spots, and a one-minute theatrical all about Terry Tate, the office linebacker," says Hein. "We shot those on 16mm, but it looks like 35mm. It looks amazing. It was shot with the intention of finding a sponsorship. At the same time, it was also shot for a showcase piece for the director. In success it can function as both."

Eduardo Rodriguez was pleasantly surprised when Florida State, where he was attending film school, got some extra money and bought brand-new 35mm cameras. "We were budgeted for 16mm, and we were going to shoot on 16mm, and after they bought the cameras, they told us, 'If you guys want to go ahead and shoot on 35mm, go for it,'" says Rodriguez. It sounded too good to be true. Then they dropped the bomb—he would have to shoot with the same budget he had for the 16mm movie. As a result, he would have to shorten the script.

Rodriguez decided to use the 35mm cameras because he thought it was going to look a lot better. "I thought it would look more professional, and we thought it was going to be good for everyone involved with the project to have a 35mm movie on their résumé instead of a 16mm film," says Rodrguez. "The script was fifteen pages, and it wasn't a big deal to take it down to twelve."

If all else fails, never be too proud to beg, barter, or borrow equipment. I know several production assistants who borrowed equipment from the film project they were working on to film with on the weekends.

Many craftsman own their own equipment and may include its usage as part of their deal, or for a nominal rental fee. If you own a piece of equipment, perhaps you can loan it out on trade with a fellow filmmaker.

THE LEAST YOU NEED

The amount of equipment you need to use is completely dependent upon the story you are telling. "Mini-DV has opened up movie-making to anybody," says cinematographer Eric Haase. "But just because it's cheap doesn't mean it's the right tool to use. I think the DV format or the video format is really appropriate for certain stories, but it's not appropriate for all stories. So if you have a very simple story that is going to be facilitated by the format of DV, then the least amount of equipment you need is a DV camera and a nonlinear editing system. You don't even need that—you can edit VCR to VCR."

That said, when Haase is shooting a film, he likes to have all the bells and whistles at his disposal if possible. "I like to have everything," admits Haase. "I like to have all the big toys. It's a lot of fun. I always prefer to shoot 35mm. High definition is coming up. In a year or two, cameras will be smaller and the latitude range of exposure will be better. It's another tool for the medium. I really enjoy working in it, and I've really enjoyed experimenting with high definition. I think it's great for certain stories right now—not for all stories. And I think eventually the types of stories it's appropriate for will expand."

Haase would consider using high definition on something that is dark where you have controlled lighting environments, like a film noir. "If you've got night interiors and night exteriors where you're going to be doing the lighting anyway, and you've got control over the locations, high definition is great," says Haase. "If you have uncontrolled day interiors where there's some light coming in, it's a little bit harder to manage the high light.

"That's where the problems come in in high definition," continues Haase. "Something like *Star Wars* [*Episode I—The Phantom Menace*], where they're very excited about shooting in high definition, everything is on a stage and it's all controlled. That's the way most of it is. There's some location stuff. I shouldn't shoot high definition on an epic period piece right now because it's just not right yet. It's a harder look. The texture is not quite right. It's not like film. There's something organic and beautiful about film. I think high definition will get there eventually, but not right now."

HELLO, DOLLY

In addition to film stock, there is other equipment that is important to be familiar with when planning your shoot. In *George Lucas in Love,* Joe Nussbaum used a lot of dollies because there was a great deal of camera movement. He also used a Steadicam. "Just like *Shakespeare in Love,* we wanted the flow," says Nussbaum. "When George Lucas walks through campus, that's a Steadicam shot. He walks out, he walks past the van, he walks around the corner, he sees the preacher yelling, he walks past the bush, and there's R2D2 and C3PO—that's all one big shot that lasts for forty seconds. I think there's one cut in it.

"Generally, with Steadicam, if you're making a short, you can usually find these guys who are on their way up who want to be Steadicam operators and own their own rig," continues Nussbaum. "All Stedicam operators generally own their own rig. When you decide that you want to be a Steadicam operator, the first thing you have to do is buy it. We got this guy for an unbelievably cheap amount of money because he wanted to put stuff on his reel."

LIGHTING

If you want your film to be lit and you want to tell your story through lighting, through color, through those deliberate choices, then you need lighting. You have the ability to correct everything later, but if you want a soft light on somebody's face, you either need to put them in a spot that has that light, or you need to light it no matter what format you choose.

The format you choose to acquire your images does not necessarily change how much lighting you are going to need. You will have the same amount of lighting for 16mm as for 35mm, or for high definition as for 35mm. For high definition, you might not have a 10k lamp, you might only have a 5k, but you still need all the 2s, the 1s, etc. If you do not want to do a lot of lighting, you do not have to do a lot of lighting.

It was a thrill for Eric Haase to light and shoot *George Lucas in Love* because it provided him a homecoming opportunity to shoot on the campus of his alma mater, USC, which also happened to be the alma mater of George Lucas himself. They even shot a scene in a classroom Haase had taken classes in.

For the short, Haase tore out a row of seats to build some dolly tracks in the back of the theater. Then he rigged a bunch of ParCan lights on the ceiling to create a backlight on the Lucas character and pools of light on the seats. A simple hard light with a flag that swung open was used to reveal the Princess Leia–like shadow on the movie screen—a screen that has undoubtedly seen many showings of *Star Wars* in its day.

SOUND OFF

Another element that is essential to your film is good sound design. You want to consider not only production sound, the dialogue and ambience you record on set, but also the sound mix later in post-production when you add sound effects, Foley, and score to the film. It is possible to dub flubbed lines through the looping process, but it is easier and more cost effective to record them the first time during production. Make sure you allocate the necessary resources for an experienced sound team.

Trevor Sands wanted to do something experimental with the ensemble performance on *Inside*. He was working with a relatively large cast and they were all onscreen at once, so he wanted to take the Robert Altman overlapping dialogue concept to an extreme. Sands did not know whether to boom his actors or to use individual wireless microphones.

"It was a big decision because I had some people telling me wireless microphones are going to be a nightmare," remembers Sands. " 'You're gonna get signals crossed. You're gonna get static. It's not going to be clean. You should just have one boom above them and make it simple.' Then I had other people telling me wireless microphones are the only way to go. 'If you try to do it boom, you're just gonna get a mess of dialogue that's not gonna make any sense. Anybody, if they're legit, be it Robert Altman in the old days or anyone else recently, they all use wireless microphones.' "

Finally, it was Eric Haase who came to the rescue. He had a relationship with Lee Orloff, a production sound mixer who had worked on such films as *The Abyss*, *Terminator 2: Judgment Day*, and *Ali*. "We got on the phone with him and asked him. He said, 'Wireless is the way to go,' " says Sands. "We were mixing it on the fly on separate tracks so that in post-production you could mix and match stuff." That is exactly what they did, and when you listen to the final mix, you can be sure they made the right decision.

Eduardo Rodriguez used a Dolby surround system for the final mix of *Daughter*. "That made a huge difference," says Rodriguez. "When she's having all those nightmares and hallucinations, those screams are actually in back of you. Also, with the cubes at the end, the screams of the people go from the back to the front of the theater. That was another thing for me that was very helpful and helped the movie in a very good way that we got that surround equipment for the final mix."

CUT

Many short film directors also act as their own editors, but that certainly is not a requirement. There are plenty of aspiring editors who would gladly work with you to edit your short film. Many of them even have access to editing equipment, like Avids, because they are working as assistant editors on larger features by day. At night, Hollywood post-houses come alive as editors work on a variety of side projects.

Eduardo Rodriguez cut *Daughter* using an Avid machine. "Nonlinear equipment is very useful because you can switch shots and scenes in a very efficient way," says Rodriguez. "That makes a big difference between cutting there or cutting on a Moviola and having to cut the film and tape it together and risk losing a piece of film that you wanted."

These days you do not even need an Avid. You can cut right at home on your personal computer. Software programs like Final Cut Pro and Adobe Premiere allow you to edit your film from the convenience of your living room. Programs like After Effects provide the capability to produce your own visual effects. The best thing about these applications is that they enable you to save a great deal of money. When you are shooting in the digital realm, it is very simple to use. If you do choose to shoot on film, you must absorb the cost of a transfer if you want to edit on your home computer.

COMPROMISE

There are a lot of choices when it comes to equipment. When making decisions about renting equipment, always think about what is necessary to make the movie versus what would be nice to use if you can afford it. Remember why you want to make the film and what you hope it will accomplish, and spend your money wisely.

For Trevor Sands, format was never a question for him when making *Inside*. From the beginning, he knew he would shoot on 35mm. His reasoning was logical. If you want to direct a feature and you want people to take you seriously, you shoot on 35mm. "We all got together and made these movies the way we would make a feature film, just with less money," says Sands. "They're just like small little features. We try to keep the quality that high. That's the goal."

5

Crew: The People Who Will Help You Achieve Your Vision

"If you surround yourself with the best people possible, it's only going to increase your chances of looking good."

—Steve Hein, producer

SHOOT TO KILL

Like many aspiring cinematographers, Eric Haase worked as a camera assistant when he graduated from film school. This is probably the most common entry-level job for someone who aspires to be a director of photography. Get experience as part of a camera crew, and gradually work your way up from loader to second assistant to first assistant to operator until you get a shot to DP yourself. But Haase was really aching to shoot. So he did what any ambitious young cinematographer right out of film school would do. He produced a few shorts so he could hire himself as director of photography, shoot them himself, and start building his reel.

One of those shorts was *Battle of the Sexes*, which Eric Kripke directed. "I would produce these short films and shoot them to start building my reel," explains Haase, who knew how to produce because he had taken a producing class in college. "I just had to go out there and shoot as much as I could. I said I'm not going to sit around and wait for someone to give me the chance to shoot their film. I know this guy wants to make a short. So I say I can produce this short and shoot it as well. That's what happened."

When it comes to creating a film—even a short film—you cannot do it all by yourself. You will need to assemble a hardworking and dedicated crew that will probably be willing to work for little to no money. This chapter is about how to find the right people to carry out your creative vision, and how to inspire them so they are as dedicated and motivated as you.

THE POWER OF ONE

Technically, a short film could be done solo. When I made my student films, I operated without a crew. It was just me, my Super 8 camera, and a bunch of actors shooting outdoors in natural light. But these early films are also filled with technical mistakes and inconsistencies, and it is not work I am overly eager to show people.

With animation, working solo is more common. The advantage of working with others is the speed with which the projects can be completed. When working alone, it just takes much longer for one person to draw and shoot each frame, or to key each sequence into the computer if they are working with CGI (computer graphics).

"Those shorts are often auteur films," says Peter Lord, whose earliest animated films were indeed films he made by himself. "When you make those sort of films at film school, you do everything yourself. It's traditional. I don't think it's sensible. I think it's a bad idea. But you do. You make the models. You write the script. You do the lighting. You do the animation. You do the editing. You do everything yourself."

And although many things have changed for Oscar-winner Lord, today he still works with a skeletal crew. "If we were doing one at work now within the studio, we'd probably do it with a crew of three or four," says Lord. "Certainly an animator, a lighting/cameraman, you'd need an electrician part-time, and model makers is another issue. But I think a crew of three or four is how we'd like it to go—a very intimate group of people, sharing jobs, doing everything. A lighting/cameraman could pick up a paint brush and paint the set."

FRIENDS

Once you reach a certain point in your career, it no longer makes sense to do it all by yourself. A hardworking crew soon becomes a necessity. Due to budgetary restrictions, oftentimes there is no money to pay the crew. That means relying on your friends to step up to the plate. If you happen to go to film school where you are surrounded by friends who are technically proficient in the mechanics of filmmaking, great. But most people do not have a group of friends who have been trained in the filmmaking process.

"Usually the people you get are your friends who are going to help you out and they're not always the most qualified technicians," says Haase. "It's going to take a little bit longer than it normally takes, but you can't take longer because you don't have the schedule because you don't have the budget, etc. It seems to be a never ending catch-22."

On the other hand, sometimes your friends are not only technically proficient, but they are also working in the business in a capacity where they can really help you out. On *Battle of the Sexes,* Haase had a friend he grew up with who was working in an online facility. "We snuck in after hours [to edit the film]," reveals Eric Kripke, the film's director. "You start working with people you meet when you're a PA, and they have friends, and they have friends, and you'll find what you need if you try hard enough."

Luke Greenfield did the same thing with *The Right Hook.* "There was an editor named Darrin Roberts who I went to film school with," says Greenfield. "Darrin helped us get an Avid for free over at *The Simpsons* where he worked. We were editing like crazy, and Darrin was cutting for free."

People are willing to work for free if they believe in the project and if they respect the leadership of the project. After all, other young, hungry filmmakers want to get experience working on set, another credit for their résumé, or some film for their reel. Everyone has to pay their dues. Today's production assistant is tomorrow's director. If the PA works on another director's film for free, one day, when that PA is directing his own film, another PA will be there to support his efforts.

"I was lucky in that on both productions, everybody worked for free," says Eric Kripke, who produced two short films, *Truly Committed* and *Battle of the Sexes,* with free labor. "I was fortunate enough to have all these hungry, young, talented people around me. We were all excited to shoot."

Ask Kripke if he could pull that feat off with the same group of people today, and he is not so optimistic. "Now everyone is actually making money and working, but at the time, we were young and hungry," says Kripke. "A great way to have a free crew is to live in Los Angeles and make friends with as many young, hungry, talented filmmakers in their early twenties as possible."

Don't just look for people who only want to direct. There are people out there who want to be editors and designers, etc. "There's an amazing talent pool of young hungry people who are working second jobs, waiting tables, and temping to pay the bills. You come to them and you're giving them an opportunity to build their reels," says Kripke. "Whether they want to be an actor or musician or DP, they're gonna want to do it, and they'll work their asses off. They'll work harder than professionals because their careers are on the line, too. That's how we crewed up."

Eduardo Rodriguez had the benefit of crewing up with his fellow students. "Five people get thesis films. The rest of the classmates who don't get to make their projects crew up on our films," explains Rodriguez.

In addition to the other students, wannabe filmmakers also need to get experience and build their reels. There is an entire community of people willing to volunteer their time for your project. "The way the system works is when you want to go to film school, when you apply, you have to show your résumé," says Rodriguez. "One of the things that makes a difference is if you have a background of volunteering for other films. A lot of people are always there who want to get into film school. They are helping people out, and they are very excited about it. So it helps you and at the same time it helps them because they have a better chance of getting into film school."

LOOKING BEYOND THE DIRECTOR'S CHAIR

Believe it or not, not everyone aspires to be a director. This is a good thing. After all, if everyone wanted to direct, who would help crew? Besides, not everyone is meant to direct. Some people have skills in a specific craft area where their talent can shine like a star. If they were to become a director, that creative muscle might not have the right opportunity to flex itself on an ongoing basis.

When Eric Haase first started film school at USC, he was not sure which craft he wanted to pursue. One of the great things about film school, however, is that it gives students an opportunity to experience all the various crafts so they can find their niche. Haase directed a short film for a class he was taking the summer between his junior and senior years. It was a ten-minute black-and-white 16mm short with dialogue. Through that experience, he realized that he enjoyed the process of shooting so much more than the other responsibilities of a director, such as working with the actors. As a result, after he finished that project, he decided he wanted to only do cinematography.

"Ever since I was a kid, I have loved looking through the camera," says Haase. "I really enjoy telling a story visually. I enjoy still photography. I enjoy the process of lighting and color. As a director, you have the opportunity to do that, but you don't get to focus only on that and make that your craft. I enjoy focusing on that."

Haase thoroughly enjoys the technical aspect of the filmmaking process. "As a director of photography, you have to understand editing. Yet you don't have to understand photography to be an editor. You can say that looks good or that doesn't look good, but you don't have to know how to get it. I have to know how to cut. I have to know how the story's going to work. I have to know how the sound design is going to fit into shooting because I need to know if a camera move should be faster or slower. What's the sound design that's going to go along with it?

"I think being a director of photography incorporates everything," says Haase. "Being a director incorporates everything, but you don't necessarily have that technical side of it that I also really enjoy. I like that hands-on feeling of it, rather than just sitting there and saying this is what I want, everybody go do it."

TEN THINGS I LOVE ABOUT CREW

Why work on a short film crew? Sure, you probably want to direct your *own* film. But sometimes, the best experience can be gleaned from helping out others with their film projects. Think of the director as the president. He must assemble the best advisers possible to help him make smart choices. The president has the members of his cabinet, the vice president, the Secretary of Defense, etc. A director's advisers are his key crew: cinematographer, editor, production designer, costume designer, etc.

There are plenty of reasons to work on a short, even if you are not the director. For starters, working on a short film can help others get a start in the industry. It is résumé-builder. More so, it is solid experience. You might go to film school and get a degree in production, but it is not the same as physically being on a set and experiencing production firsthand.

Working on other people's shorts is also a great networking opportunity. You will meet others who share your passion for filmmaking—after all, that is the reason they are on set as well. These fellow crew members might become valuable contacts, alerting you to employment opportunities and other prospects of interest to you.

Being on set is a great place for observation. You can truly see how each and every person does his or her job and how the various crew positions interact to make movie magic. Even if you are working as a production assistant, this is an opportunity to perhaps find your niche within the filmmaking process. Watch, listen, ask a lot of questions, and learn as much as you can just by being there.

Finally, if you do plan to direct your own short one day, there is no better experience than being a part of the process on someone else's short film. Do not go into your own film project blindly. There is too much on the line. Get the experience you need before undertaking the task yourself.

Another reason to volunteer to work on a crew is to get the opportunity to experiment with various techniques. "If you are a cinematographer and you're going to shoot a short film, the most important thing is to experiment and learn from it, and not to say this is the short that's going to launch my career," says Eric Haase. "If you approach it like that, you're just setting yourself up for disappointment. On the other hand, if you say these are the things I want to learn and accomplish and experiment with on this film, then you will be getting the most out of the experience.

"On *Battle of the Sexes,* I wanted to try a certain type of camera movement because I'd never done it before," continues Haase. "I wanted to do some handheld work. I wanted to use some red and some blue and try and get these colors to work together and use some flashing lights—the kind of stuff I'd never done before. I wanted to give the bar scene a different look, a warmer look, a whiter light as opposed to the bathroom, which is more science-fiction/*Crimson Tide.* I wanted to try out these styles. So you try out different things you're interested in photographically and eventually you find your own voice, you find your own style of things that you like to do, that you're better at, or things that you don't necessarily like. You develop your taste.

"As a cinematographer, experiment, find your style, find your taste, find your voice," says Haase. "Don't expect that I'm gonna shoot this, this guy's gonna make it, he's gonna bring me along, and we're gonna be huge and famous after doing one thing together. It takes a long time to foster those relationships. Try to develop real working relationships with the director you work with."

Does owning your own equipment give you a leg up on getting a job on the crew? "I think what's most important is that they be talented people and that they be good and share your vision for the movie," suggests Eric Kripke. "We never brought on anyone because they could bring something to the table. On other productions, those people have been brought on and they almost invariably turn out to be [no good].

"You need to bring on someone you get along with and like and then you'll find a way to get the equipment," continues Kripke. "The same guy who's a brilliant editor who had to rent these big bulky drives to cut *Battle of the Sexes* just won an MTV Video Award for a video he edited on his Apple computer laptop. So I don't think equipment should really be a consideration anymore, especially post equipment, because I think so much of it is readily accessible."

MASTER AND COMMANDER

One thing that is always important, particularly if you are working with an unpaid crew, is the ability of the director to command respect. That comes in many forms. For one, treat people the way you want to be treated. An easy way to lose your crew is to scream at and belittle them. Instead, be respectful. When appropriate, make a point to acknowledge good work.

Feed your crew well. This is one of the oldest tricks in the book, but if you have great craft services on set, you will have a happy crew. "They will get tired, and that's the one thing you can do to take care of everybody," says producer Steve Hein. "Make sure they're well fed and there's plenty of coffee. If your movie stinks and you're not feeding everybody every six hours, they'll get cranky." Crews that are well fed are more likely to work with the greatest efficiency even when the days go long.

Remember, production can be so unpredictable. Shooting days can run close to fourteen hours. "And you will go overtime," warns Hein. "Don't fool anybody into thinking they're going to be working ten-hour days when you know you're going to be working fifteen. Make them aware when you're hitting hour twelve and you know you're going to be working eighteen hours. Tell everyone. Don't let them think they're getting out of there in an hour. It's communication. It's trying to take care of your guys especially when more than likely they're working for free."

Make your passion contagious. "If your project is really good, the material is there, and you're passionate about it, then part of being a short filmmaker is getting other people passionate about the material, too," says Gary Bryman. When the crew sees your enthusiasm take over, they will be completely onboard with whatever you want to do. When hiring people, find key crew who share your vision for the material. If someone is as passionate as you are about the screenplay, think how hard they will work to help bring the story to fruition.

Finally, be the hardest worker on the set. When the crew sees that you are working just as hard as everyone else, they will continue to give it their all. Just because you are the director does not mean you cannot help out during down time. On low-budget, independent projects, diving into the trenches with your crew is a sure way to show them you are not afraid to get your hands dirty.

"One of the things I think was great about our crew and that made my job a lot easier is that most of the people knew what kind of films I made because all my other films are horror movies," says Rodriguez. "The people who were working there knew what they were getting into, and they were excited about the project. They believed in the project. Also, the people who were there were inspired by themselves because they believed in the project and they wanted to make a good movie. And that made my job a lot easier because the people who worked with me were already inspired by the project itself."

BEST CREW MONEY CAN BUY

If you can afford to do so, there is a benefit to paying your crew. No matter how much passion you have, and no matter how great the food might be, nothing speaks louder and clearer than cold, hard cash. The main advantage in having the ability to hire a crew is that you are likely to get people with more experience. And if you are a first-time director, the more experienced the crew, the better off you will be.

"You should get the best crew possible," says Steve Hein. "If you have a weak AD [assistant director], guess what? Your set is going to be slow. If you have first-time sound guy, guess what? You're sound's going to suck. It's not the time, when you're spending this much money and you're looking for this much opportunity, to necessarily be taking risks on other people. You're going to try and get as many people around you to compensate for the fact that you might not have that much experience."

"I tried to do everything as well as it could be done, which is why it ended up costing so much, because I decided I wasn't going to cut corners," says *Inside* director Trevor Sands. "I was not going to short-change the process. I wanted this to be a legitimate shoot, and I wanted everyone involved to feel good about being a part of it. For me, it was worth spending the extra ten to fifteen thousand dollars it cost to do that because I really think it does affect the final project in terms of the quality of work you get from everyone, how quickly you can do what you need to do, and the overall vibe of the set. If everybody's pissed off and angry that they're even there and working toward the fifteenth hour on this miserable set, I would be surprised if the material you're getting is as good as it can be. I'd been on enough fiasco film sets and been on enough low-budget shoots to realize that when you have enough money to treat people right and to do things right and to get all the tools you need, that things actually can go pretty smoothly."

Sometimes you might be able to hire experienced people for less than they usually make. "When you're hiring professional union people, the set actually works," continues Sands. "It was not an official union shoot, but we did have a lot of union people, and they graciously took for instance, maybe half of their union rate, but we did pay people a reasonable amount of money for their time. It wasn't fifty-dollar-a-day kind of stuff. I think people were getting paid between a hundred and four hundred dollars a day, depending on their position."

"A lot of times, it's the passion of the filmmaker going to the right people and just sort of pleading their case," says Gary Bryman. "And if for some reason it seems like it's a worthwhile endeavor, people will work for less than they're entitled to. Everyone is sort of looking at the same thing—a really good project to be involved in. So if you're fortunate enough to have that idea and you can go around and sell it, then you're in a pretty good position."

Mike Mitchell was able to call on a lot of his industry contacts for favors while making his short film, *Herd*. "Lance Henrickson was the director of photography who worked for free," says Mitchell. "I used to do storyboards for Spike Jonze, and he shot a few Spike Jonze videos. I got favors from all my animator friends—guys to build models and help me out. [Model maker] Andrew Jones built the puppets for free."

Luke Greenfield had been editing *The Right Hook* for a while when he began searching for Joe Hutshing, an editor whose name he kept seeing on all of his favorite edited movies. "Joe Hutshing was one of the biggest editors in town," says Greenfield. "He cut *Jerry Maguire, JFK, The Doors,* and so I hunted him down and showed him the rough cut of my film. Amazingly, he volunteered to help me fine-tune it with his associate, Mark Livolsi, who's the editor I'm working with now."

Bryan Gordon approached some high-profile filmmakers when crewing up for *Ray's Male Heterosexual Dance Hall*. He asked veteran cinematographer Philip Lathrup to shoot his short film. "I didn't want to shoot it like an MTV film," recalls Gordon. "I always admired *They Shoot Horses, Don't They?* because I wanted to base the film on people dancing in a very simple way and shoot it simply. I looked up the DP on that film and found that it was Philip Lathrup."

Gordon called up the semi-retired Lathrup to solicit his advice on how to shoot the film and somehow managed to convince the veteran cinematographer to shoot it. "He brought with him a white-haired crew," says Gordon. "They came all dressed up in suits because when they started out, people dressed in coat and tie on set. From that moment on, I have gained so much respect for people who have experience."

PARTY OF TWO, TABLE FOR ONE

We talk a lot about short films being a director's medium, and to a great extent this is true. You never read that the production designer of a short film just got a three-picture deal with the studio. You read that the director of that film got the deal instead. But would it not make sense that if indeed the director of a short got a studio deal, that he would hire his production team onto the feature?

"It's difficult because the studios say it's a first-time director, so we have to go with an experienced director of photography who will be able to bring it in on schedule and on budget," says Eric Haase, who never expects to be hired onto the features of the directors whose shorts he photographed. "They will always fight for me. Joe Nussbaum had fought for me to get in on these screen tests. That went very well. The line producer asked, 'When are you available to shoot this movie?' We were going to talk about it more seriously, but the movie never happened."

According to producer Jana Sue Memel, "All filmmaking is a collaboration. I've made eighty-one films between the shorts, cable movies, documentaries, and rock videos, and I've worked in almost every filmmaking medium. For better or worse, filmmaking is the penultimate collaborative medium because if a department lets you down, it shows. It's a directors' medium in the sense that the director has to make the ultimate decision. But it's the most collaborative medium because their decisions are based on the choices presented to them by others, most importantly the cinematographer and the production designer.

"When you're sitting there with a chisel and a bunch of stone, that's a directors' medium. Even brushes and paint," continues Memel. "But in filmmaking, you're ultimately making decisions. And so it's a directors' medium to the extent that you make the right decisions, and you inspire the people around you to deliver the things that will make you look good. It's absolutely the most collaborative medium around."

Hang in there. These relationships are extremely valuable. And one day, in the not too distant future, either you or the director will be in a position to mandate that you work together.

CREATIVE CREWING

Like every other aspect of filmmaking, be creative and resourceful when putting together a crew. Eduardo Rodriguez needed someone who was proficient with special effects makeup for his horror short *Daughter*. There was nobody at his school who could provide the realistic blood and guts he desperately needed to pull off his gags.

"In Orlando there are a couple makeup schools," says Rodriguez who, along with the film's producers, started contacting the schools one by one to see if they could find a makeup artist who could do the job. "We got this guy from the makeup school. I always call him the Corpse Grinder. He came with his girlfriend, and they did all the blood and special effects makeup. It looks so real."

One of the challenges on *Truly Committed* was sneaking twenty musicians from USC's music school into the film school's Spielberg scoring stage to record the film's score. They had to sneak in because at the time, Kripke had graduated a few years before and was no longer a student. "It's very funny to sneak in with thirty-odd people, getting everyone into the door," says Kripke. "We brought in a mixer to work on the equipment. We had to station PAs around the film school to make sure the faculty wasn't coming."

Whatever it takes to get the job done, that's what you need to do. Hopefully, you will find the best people possible to help you realize your vision to its maximum potential. As you will see in the next chapter, the crew are not the only people who will help bring your film to life. Having a well-prepared and supportive cast is also a vital element of the filmmaking process.

6

Cast: Finding Actors to Bring Your Script to Life

"The key to putting together a great cast is pretty simple. Find the best actors available who can bring the most to the role. If an actor can do a part just how you pictured it in your head, that's great. But if they can do it better than you pictured it with choices and nuances you hadn't thought of, that's even better."

—Joe Nussbaum, director

BEFORE THEY WERE STARS

Everybody has to start somewhere, and short films are a win-win for aspiring actors. They are a great way to get some experience on set, get credits on their résumé, get tape for their reel, and develop relationships with the filmmakers of tomorrow. You might be amazed to find out how many of today's successful actors began their careers working on short films.

At USC, I cast in one of my student films a young actor who had no credits whatsoever. But I took a chance on this untested thespian, and he ended up doing a great job. After I finished my movie, I got busy with other projects and I lost touch with him.

A couple years later, I was working on the TV show *Love Connection* auditioning contestants to be on the show. Who did I bump into in the waiting room, filling out an application to be a contestant? That same young actor. Sorry to say, he did not get chosen to be on the program.

A few more years went by. I was living in the Valley, trying to decide what to do for dinner. I order a pizza. Thirty minutes later the doorbell rings, and who do you think the pizza boy was? The same actor. I asked how the acting was going. He was still hanging in there, trying to make it happen. I think that is great.

About two years later, I was at the premiere of the film *Citizen Ruth*. The party was being held at the famous Chateau Marmont. As I made my way around the room, I bumped into that same young actor. I approached him and said hello, and asked the usual questions. This time, he sounded a bit more upbeat. He told me he just appeared in a movie for the guy who directed those *Nightmare on Elm Street* movies.

Of course, that director was Wes Craven. The movie was *Scream*. And the young actor who got his start in my short film was Jamie Kennedy. Kennedy continues to enjoy a very successful career in Hollywood. After roles in more than a dozen feature films, he is the star of his own successful television program, *The Jamie Kennedy Experiment*. And to think, he got his start in a short.

CAST ME IF YOU CAN

Casting is an integral part of the filmmaking process. And although it is possible to cast your short by yourself, it is highly recommended that you hire a casting director to assist you in this task. Like any other crew member, you might be able to get a casting director to work for little or no money. Oftentimes, professional casting assistants or casting associates will volunteer their time to cast independent shorts to build up their own résumé with casting director credits.

One of the best-cast shorts is *George Lucas in Love*. The two leads were actors whom director Joe Nussbaum knew, but the supporting players were assembled by casting director, Jeremy Jones, who did an amazing job finding actors to parody the characters in *Star Wars* iconography.

Lisa Jakub was cast as the Princess Leia–inspired Miriam. She had been working professionally as an actor, appearing in such films as *Mrs. Doubtfire*, *Independence Day*, and *Rambling Rose*. Tim Dowling, who had shared story by credit on the film, had co-starred with Jakub in the feature *The Beautician and the Beast*. "We asked her to do it, and she said she would, which was amazing," says Nussbaum.

Finding their George Lucas was a critical task, but they could not have done better than actor Martin Hynes. Hynes had been a graduate student at USC while Nussbaum was earning his undergraduate degree. Hynes had made a graduate thesis film that he had written, directed, and starred in that Nussbaum had seen. "Once I saw him onscreen, I knew he was exactly the guy I was looking for—a young George Lucas meets Woody Allen," says Nussbaum, who set out to contact the actor.

"Martin is very smart, very classy, and very creative, and he was like, 'Well, send me the script,'" says Nussbaum. He sent Hynes the script to read, and after reading it, Hynes agreed to meet with Nussbaum. "We meet and he says, 'Why don't you give me your student films.' He just wanted to make sure he wasn't getting involved in something that was gonna be a hellish experience and come out crappy, which is what happens with a lot of short projects."

Another connection Nussbaum made during school was Jones, who had been in the theater school at USC and who had done casting at the Mark Taper Forum and then at Fox. "We asked him to cast our movie," recalls Nussbaum. Jones agreed and he cast the remainder of the roles. "He either auditioned just a couple people for the roles, or didn't audition anyone. He just said, 'Here's who's doing it. I'm going to ask Patrick Kerr to play Yoda, and if he says yes, he's doing it.' Jeremy couldn't have been more right about everyone."

THE STAR

It certainly is not inconceivable to land a well-known star in your short film. Basically it comes down to the material. After all, actors are always looking for great roles that will help them stretch and grow in their craft. Sometimes these great opportunities are in the form of independent shorts.

Trevor Sands cast Jeremy Sisto, one of the stars of *Six Feet Under*, as the lead in his short film *Inside*. He had known Sisto through friends and had actually cast him years before in one of his student productions. "When it came time to shoot *Inside*, I thought he would be good for it," says Sands. "I tracked down his number and called him on his cell phone. He was on the set of *Six Feet Under* and we chatted briefly. He said he'd take a look at my script and very quickly called me back and said 'Let's do it.'"

Having a star in your film is not necessary, but it will certainly bring more attention to your project. It will have a leg up on its competition for getting into film festivals because just like in features, stars get bodies into the theaters. But remember, now that more attention is being focused on your movie, make sure every other aspect of the production is above par as well.

STAR SEARCH

There is no shortage of actors in Los Angeles and New York. But what if you are trying to make a short film outside of one of these major cities? How do you cast it? That is exactly the dilemma Eduardo Rodriguez was in when the Florida State University student was looking to cast his short film *Daughter*.

Tallahassee is not exactly thought of as a hotbed for rising new talent. And although Rodriguez could have drawn actors from the talent pool at the school's theater department, that offered somewhat of a limited selection. Instead, the Venezuelan native got together with his fellow student directors to conduct a five-city talent search encompassing Tampa, Orlando, Miami, Tallahassee, and Atlanta.

"All five thesis producers and directors got together and we made a list of what kind of actors we were looking for," says Rodriguez. "We talked to some local talent agencies to set up some casting calls. They sent over head shots and we did a pre-selection in Tallahassee and then we told them the ones we wanted to see, and they set up a casting call for us."

It was in Atlanta that Rodriguez found both actors he ultimately cast in his short. Marcie Seklecki was the first actor he met with. "She wasn't *the one* as soon as I saw her, but she was one of the ones I wanted to call back because she was very good," says Rodriguez. She ultimately was cast in the role of Shae Powell, the single mom who wakes up in hell after having murdered her daughter.

Six-year-old Jennifer Ashlyn Qualey, who played the title character in Rodriguez's short, made a great first impression on the director. "One of the things she had going for her was she wasn't shy at all," says Rodriguez. "I thought that was going to make a very big difference, because at that age I don't know that you can have too much acting skill, especially for a little girl who doesn't have any experience. One of the most important things for me was to find a little girl who wasn't going to freeze in front of the camera."

Qualey, who bears an eerie resemblance to Heather O'Rourke, the actress who played the young girl, Carol Anne, in *Poltergeist,* almost did not get the role. "The production designer didn't want to cast her because he said people are going to say that you're trying to get the little girl from *Poltergeist,*" says Rodriguez. "I thought that was a good thing to have. For me, she was exactly like the little girl from *Poltergeist* and that was a scary movie, so I thought that was a good reference to have. I didn't think it was going to affect the movie in a bad way."

Another reason these actors were cast was because they had a very positive attitude about working on the student film. This is as important as everything else when making your casting decisions. Because the actors are working for free or very little money, you have to be sure they are onboard through thick and thin. "They were all excited about doing the movie," says Rodriguez. "They were very much into making a movie. I think that's very important. You have people there who want to cooperate and believe in the project. It can be very challenging. If you don't care about the project, you're not going to give it too much of your talent, and I don't think that's the way it should be. So for me they were the perfect casting, and I'm very thankful for that."

Now that Rodriguez had found his cast, there was one more challenge: how to get the actors from Atlanta to Tallahassee, and where to house them once they were at the Florida location. "We got the hotels for free," says Rodriguez, who was able to convince a local hotel to donate a free room to the production. "In Tallahassee, the community knows the film school is there so they cooperate a lot. Marcie was staying with a woman who always opens her house to people while we're shooting films."

WORKING WITH SAG ACTORS

Professional actors are members of the Screen Actors Guild (SAG). This union protects the rights of actors through various efforts such as setting a minimum wage for the provision of services. Because it would be cost-prohibitive to employ SAG actors on low-budget shorts and other independent films, SAG has created several different low-budget contracts enabling their members to work on these projects for reduced or deferred wages. As a filmmaker, you should be aware of the various contracts and the rules that garner each one.

The SAG agreement summaries for experimental films (under $75,000) and student films can be found online at www.sag.org. In order to qualify your production for either of these contracts, you must submit a letter to SAG outlining your project's parameters. One such letter follows.

WILL ACT FOR FOOD

Many times, actors do not get paid for shorts because they qualify as SAG experimental films. Sometimes payment is deferred and the actors receive

SCREEN ACTORS GUILD

May 10, 2001
Theatrical Contracts

Trevor Sands
5555 Wilshire Blvd.
Los Angeles, CA 90036

Re: Film entitled: "Inside"

Dear Experimental/Student Filmmaker:

This letter is in response to your inquiry concerning requirements of the Screen Actors Guild for filmmakers who would like to use Screen Actors Guild members for EXPERIMENTAL or STUDENT films. The following information must be submitted for consideration to work under the experimental/student film agreement:

EXPERIMENTAL AND STUDENT

- a. Type of contract (Experimental or Student).
- b. Project title.
- c. Owner of the film.
- d. Medium to be used.
- e. Intention for producing this project.
- f. Intended use of the film upon completion.
- g. By whom the project is financed.
- h. Start date.
- i. Completion date.
- j. Edited running time.
- k. Total budget (including crew deferrals).

l. Detailed budget breakdown.

m. Number of Screen Actors Guild members to be used.

n. Number of Non-Screen Actors Guild members to be used.

STUDENTS ONLY

o. Educational institution, course, and number.

p. Describe course requirements fulfilled by this project.

q. Letter of Confirmation of enrollment from instructor.

This information must be received by the Guild at least three (3) weeks prior to actual production. The information will then be reviewed to determine whether it will qualify under the Experimental/Student Film Agreement guidelines.

Upon approval, the appropriate Experimental/Student Film packet will be forwarded to you. This must be completed and returned to the Guild as soon as possible. PLEASE NOTE THAT PROOF OF THREE MONTHS MINIMUM WORKER'S COMPENSATION INSURANCE WILL BE REQUIRED. Also attatched is a Form PA which must be completed and sent along with two (2) copies of your screenplay and a thirty dollar registration fee to the United States Copyright office. Please retain a copy of the completed Form PA and proof of mailing to submit to the Guild.

If you have any questions, please do not hesitate to contact me at 323-555-5555.

Sincerely,

Ari A. Zeltzer
Business Representative, Theatrical Contracts

INSIDE

May 11, 2001

Ari A. Zeltzer
Business Representative, Theatrical Contracts
5757 Wilshire Blvd.
Los Angeles, CA 90036

Dear Ari,

I am writing to you to apply for an experimental project currently entitled INSIDE by Trevor Sands. Trevor is the writer/director and the project and the individual who will be financing and therefore owning the film. We plan on shooting the film on 35mm. The short is being produced to showcase Trevor's skills as a director. We plan to showcase the film at film festivals and other appropriate venues for a film of this nature. We plan to start shooting the film on June 1 and wrapping photography on June 3. We plan on having the entire project completed by July 30. The total running time of the project is 8 minutes. The budget is $30,000.00.

As we are currently casting the project, the exact number of SAG members and non-SAG members is not know at this time. However, we plan on casting a total number of 12 actors. Our workers comp is currently being processed and I plan to forward you proof of that when it arrives.

Thank you for your time. If you have any questions I can be reached at 323-555-5555.

Kind regards

Steven Hein
Producer

5555 Wilshire Blvd.
Los Angeles, CA 90036
323-555-0000 FAX: 323-555-0000

money only if and when the film makes a profit. Such was the case on *Inside*. But often, when actors are starting off, or if they just really believe in the project, they are willing to work under these conditions.

"Luckily, they all agreed to do the performances on deferral," says Trevor Sands of the actors cast in his short *Inside*. "If I ever see any money from the film, I have to pay the actors. Jeremy [Sisto], too—I didn't pay him anything. Most of the other actors were young actors who knew who Jeremy was and respected him. I think people had a sense that it was going to be worth their time to be a part of it, particularly when it was only a few days.

"I tried to create a compelling atmosphere where people were having fun and felt like they were creatively engaged and they weren't just being used as props," continues Sands. "Part of it has to do with how you present a project to people and the way you're able to articulate what you want to do to get people excited about it and make them feel that this is a worthwhile effort."

REHEARSAL OF FORTUNE

Casting was a crucial part of making *Inside* work effectively. Finding the right actors to play Jeremy Sisto's multiple personalities was part of the key to making the gag work. "The most difficult part of it was the blocking," says director Trevor Sands. "Getting it right so that take to take people weren't doing things that were so wildly different that it wouldn't cut together.

"They were actually really good at going through it step by step," continues Sands. "There were certainly points where I was able to say go nuts and do whatever you want, they would just collectively talk, and we would just shoot snippets. And at other points I would have everyone stay quiet except the actor who was featured in the shot so the people in the background were pretending to talk, while in fact they weren't, and I'd be getting clean dialogue from one of the individual actors."

Soliciting flawless performances was achieved through rehearsing the cast prior to filming. "We did two evenings of rehearsal, blocking it out and making sure it was going to work," says Sands. "I didn't even know if it was going to work until I saw it because the risk going in was with everyone talking, it was just gonna be a muddled mess and it was gonna be too confusing and you were not gonna hear anyone individually. And certainly at one point in the movie it is that way because I wanted it that way. Even early on, you'll notice that there's a lot of people stepping on each other with their lines, and that's traditionally technically not something you're supposed to do, but I rehearsed it a couple times and I decided this was gonna work."

For Bryan Gordon, rehearsals were not only a big part of the production process for *Ray's Male Heterosexual Dance Hall,* they were also integral to the selection process. "The most interesting thing about the rehearsal process was that some guys were not comfortable dancing with each other," says Gordon. "And it had to portray a very straight, heterosexual feeling.

"In the rehearsal process and the audition process, we weeded out a lot of people who just couldn't dance with each other," continues Gordon. "I remember going to a place to get the other dancers, some kind of club where they did ballroom dancing, and at an intermission, asking a number of men if they'd like to be in a short film and they all raised their hands. And I said, 'Here's the other part of it: You're all going to be dancing with each other.' They were not that thrilled. But they accepted the joke and the fact that Columbia Pictures was behind it at the time [helped]."

UNDERSTUDY

You have to be prepared for anything in independent filmmaking. Sometimes actors do not show up when they are supposed to. When I was making my student film, that is exactly what happened to me. The scene took place around the dinner table where a young man was being seduced under the table by his aunt as he sat next to his unsuspecting mother. The actress who was cast as the aunt never made it to set. I had to think on my feet and come up with a reasonable solution. Because the characters were sisters, I decided to have the actress playing the mom do both roles. I had the actress switch outfits and style her hair differently for each role. Then I shot the scene so all three actors were never seen in the same shot. It actually turned out better than I had planned.

There is a scene in Eric Kripke's short *Truly Committed* where the hero pulls over a car that is being driven by an old lady. He drags her out of the vehicle and throws her onto the street. "We were in Lancaster, an hour and a half out of town, at one in the morning and our lady didn't show up," says Kripke. "She's not there. What the hell do we do? So [producer] Gary Bryman called his grandmother and got her out of bed. And it wasn't like 'Come to Santa Monica.' She had to get in her car and drive ninety minutes into the desert so we could shoot a scene. But she did it and got out there at two-thirty in the morning to shoot the scene." At least they used a stunt double to throw her out of the car!

A STAR IS BORN

Long before Matt Damon and Ben Affleck wrote *Good Will Hunting* as a piece to help launch their acting careers, another young actor was working on a short film to launch his own acting career. That actor was Vin Diesel.

Diesel wrote, directed, and starred in the short film *Multi-Facial*. The autobiographical short centered around Diesel's problems getting cast in films and television because of his ethnic appearance. The film turned out so well that it was invited to screen at the Cannes Film Festival.

At the festival, Steven Spielberg saw the short and created the role of Private Carpazo for the young actor in *Saving Private Ryan*. Subsequently, Diesel also wrote, starred in, and directed a feature-length movie, *Strays,* which screened at the Sundance Film Festival. But it was really *Ryan* that launched Diesel's professional acting career, and he has been going strong ever since.

If you are an actor waiting for your big break, you could write and direct your own short film to showcase your talents. You could also align yourself with writers and directors and collaborate on a piece for you to star in. In either case, you do not have to be completely passive, waiting around for the right role to come to you. Be a go-getter and create opportunities yourself.

HOW TO WIN AN ACTOR IN TEN DAYS

So you want to land that star in your film, but you just do not know how. Or you have found the best person for the role, but you need to convince them why they should work for two weeks for no money. What is a director to do?

Actors respond to a few things: money. Well, chances are you are not paying anything substantial, so let's move on to the next one.

Great material. There is no doubt about it, if you have got a strong story, a well-executed screenplay, a phenomenal idea, you will have your choice of actors—guaranteed.

Finally, and most important, sell actors with your passion. Make a heartfelt plea to an actor on why they are perfect for the role and how you can help them shine in the part. Once they see how devoted and committed you are to making the movie happen, if you do your job right, they will happily come onboard the project.

7

Action!: The Set Comes to Life Once the Camera Rolls

"I love problems on shoots because they force you to get creative."

—Eric Kripke, writer/director

SHOOT FOR THE MOON

Some people ask, why make a short when you can make a feature film instead? If you have the money and the resources to mount a full-length production, is investing your time and energy into a short just delaying the inevitable?

Having never sat behind the wheel of a car, would you race in the Indianapolis 500 your first time out of the gate? Having never stepped foot inside a kitchen, would you suddenly prepare a four-course meal? Then why, having never stepped behind the camera, would you make a feature film your first time out?

Trevor Sands made this critical mistake the first time he raised money to make a film. When Sands first moved to Los Angeles to attend film school at USC, all he could think about was making movies. He was a bit disheartened when he discovered that for the first two years of college, he would not have the opportunity to make films. In order to be on set, Sands volunteered to help some of the upperclassmen who were making their films.

Through these experiences, Sands formed a strong bond with fellow student Samer Daboul. Daboul, who was a few years older than Sands, was shooting one of his films, and Sands showed up to play one of the extras. "We started chatting, and from there I basically joined forces with him and helped him out on all his student films," says Sands.

By the end of Sand's freshman year, he and Daboul had scraped together about $25,000 to make an independent film. "That started what became a feature film that we made together when I was nineteen years old, which I wrote and co-directed with him," says Sands. "It sort of ballooned into a two-hundred-thousand-dollar B-movie.

"It was not money well spent," admits Sands. "The choices were not the best choices to make. The script was not ready. It was really a first draft of the first feature script I actually completed. It came together rather hastily and rather quickly. It was shot in twenty-four days. Considering the circumstances, it turned out pretty well. But ultimately, it is not something I can use to get work."

At the end of the day, you are only as good as your last film. If you make a short to launch your career and the reception is lukewarm, then you can make another short. If you make a feature and receive similar feedback, do you really think you will be able to raise money to do another?

"That was part of the learning process," says Sands. "It felt legitimate and gave me the impression of 'wow, this is easy, and at age nineteen I'm gonna make a movie and it's gonna get into festivals and I'm off and running.' But because I was so young, because I hadn't really tested the waters at all in Los Angeles, I don't think it turned out as well as it could have."

"That being said, I learned so much from the experience," admits Sands. "Not only the shooting of it, which were a very intense few weeks, but also the post-production, which dragged on for over a year because we ran out of money and had to raise more. I blindly jumped into this project and did not realize the significance of the commitment involved. It became this ongoing project that kept sucking my time and energy and focus. Instead of experiencing film school as a college student and having fun with friends and getting drunk on the weekends and sort of being a young guy, I was trying to be an adult filmmaker. My age and lack of experience contradicted that. So in a way, I shortchanged myself.

"On the flip side, I was getting tremendous insight into all the aspects of making a movie as well as all the aspects of selling a movie because we did end up getting distribution and being involved in foreign sales," says Sands. "There were plenty of shady characters I met and plenty of wacky antics that ensued once we had the finished film and once it looked fairly decent. We sort of caught the tail end of the boom in the foreign sales market, where you shoot a movie for a couple hundred grand and in those days, it would gross quite a bit of money in foreign sales. Things have since changed, and we got very lucky to make any money back at all. But it did make a little money."

The film was released domestically on video under the title *Suicide Ride,* but at the time it was called *Finding Interest.* At the end of the day, although Sands does not regret making the feature, he would not do it again. "If I was going to give advice to someone who is nineteen or twenty years old and happens to get an opportunity to make a feature, think twice about it. Or maybe think long and hard about what you're getting into and how you plan to spend your time for the next couple years," advises Sands. This is why five years after the fact, Sands went back to the drawing board to do what he should have done in the first pace—make a short film.

"I don't know why anyone starting out would jump into doing a feature," says Mike Mitchell, short-film turned feature director whose credits include *Deuce Bigalow: Male Gigolo* and *Surviving Christmas.* "Shorts are the best way to play around and practice and see if things are working without spending loads and loads of money. Especially now, when you can make a short film without even leaving your living room. You can just shoot it on video and edit it on your computer."

That said, the same planning that goes into making a feature must be done for a short film. This chapter will look at various factors you need to consider during the production of your movie. Among the topics we will discuss are scheduling, locations, and stretching the dollar.

SCHEDULING FOR DOLLARS

One thing that makes life easier on set is limiting the number of location changes. Every time you make a company move, you have to pack up the trucks, drive to the new location, and set up shop all over again. This is a big time drain. When you are working with small budgets and limited time, the last thing you want to do is keep moving the company to a new location. Try setting your story in a static location or a single place that has multiple settings.

Jana Sue Memel strongly subscribes to this philosophy. "The best short is what I call an institutional short," says Memel. "That's partly because it's the most economic. Set something somewhere—it can be a school, a hospital, a home, a boatyard—where that location has a number of different sets within it so you're not required to have a transportation department.

"Take whatever your schedule is, whether it's three days or three weeks, and make sure there is a day somewhere else that involves a fair amount of extras so you give it a sense of scope without paying the bucks to have scope," Memel continues. "The one thing that kills a short film schedule is constantly moving your unit. Devise the story around an environment, whatever that environment is, STAY THERE! That takes the time pressure off. Making your day is key, and not having to make it back to the truck, load them, go across town and unload them allows you to make your day."

Memel produced Bryan Gordon's short, *Ray's Male Heterosexual Dance Hall*, which follows this strategy to a T. "I realized it was a containable piece and given the economics, that it was important to design something so that when I submitted it, I knew it was something that could be shot," says Gordon. "You can write a great short film but have nineteen million locations and get killed." In Gordon's short, there are two locations: the dance hall, where the bulk of the movie takes place, and the park, which is crawling with extras.

Truly Committed was a truly hectic shoot because the filmmakers had twenty-one locations to shoot in eleven days. "We had a crew move every single day, which is exhausting," says director Eric Kripke. "Because we were always undermanned and we were just a bunch of kids, we would unload the trucks in the morning, we'd run cable, and we'd load cable up at night. Every day, stop shooting, load up the trucks, go to another location, unload, shoot, etc. And we were doing all that ourselves."

The cast and crew of *Truly Committed* were indeed truly committed to the project. "The actors were working fourteen-hour days. We were working nineteen-hour days for eleven days straight," says Kripke. "For some reason we thought it was better to do all the days in a row rather than just doing weekends, which makes a lot more sense. Equipment is always cheaper if you're willing to go Friday through Monday. Working consecutive weekends, makes a lot more sense. Then you can work your ass off on the weekends and rest up during the week. We went eleven days and were only sleeping two hours every night. By the end it felt like that Nam/*Apocalypse Now* experience where we're all dazed.

"When you make a short film you sort of take on this pirate mentality that you'll do anything it takes to get your shots off," he says. "Some of the stuff on *Truly Committed* was shot guerrilla style. Some of it was lacking the necessary paperwork." The bigger your crew, the more conspicuous you become, the more necessary it is to have the required permits to film on location. You can always take a chance and film without a permit, but what consequence would getting shut down have on your ability to finish the movie?

Eduardo Rodriguez had a nine-day schedule to shoot *Daughter.* He also had two additional days for pick-up shots. By all standards, that is a very generous shooting schedule. Still, it never feels like there is enough time to get every shot done that you set out to do. "You always start getting behind schedule no matter what you do," says Rodriguez. "When that happens, you have to start making decisions of what to cut out."

BARGAINING FOR LOCATIONS

Most films today are not shot inside a Hollywood soundstage, but instead are filmed on location all over the world. Rather than re-create a sand dune–rich desert, we shot *The Four Feathers* in the actual deserts of Morocco. There is no snow in Southern California, so we shot *Reindeer Games* in Northern Vancouver, where the natural resources worked in our favor. You can shoot your short film on location, too.

Battle of the Sexes was shot in only two days entirely on location. "We were lucky because we got the Century Plaza Hotel in Century City to let us have it for free," says Eric Kripke. "I hate to keep playing the USC card, but the woman who was in charge was a USC alum. She said if this was a student film, she could give it to us for free. So we did it as a student film. I had technically graduated, but a lot of people on the crew were students."

The location was perfect for what they needed. "They had this banquet area that had a bar and an adjacent bathroom and it was all sealed off from the rest of the hotel so we had almost our own little studio with every location that we needed—the bathroom and the bar," says Kripke. "Also, *Battle of the Sexes* is a little more contained movie. So we shot for two days. I think the first day was very civilized. The first day was all the stuff out in the bar. The second day was the bathroom. It got cramped and hot for sure because we were in this bathroom with all these lights, especially stylized lighting. I think we had a really long day, but one long day is no big thing. It's the eleven long days in a row that get exhausting."

Sometimes, filmmakers can look a bit closer to home when searching for a location to film. *Truly Committed* opens in a very stylized house. Eric Kripke and company really wanted to build the set, but they just didn't have the money. Then producer Gary Bryman's mother offered her own house and told the filmmakers they could paint it. "We moved all her furniture out and we brought in all this prop furniture," says Kripke. "We painted the walls. One wall was shocking pink. One wall was canary yellow. 'You guys are going to paint this back, right?' We were like, 'Oh yeah, sure.' We were young and busy and rushing off, shooting our other stuff. And this poor woman is left with her house like this for weeks and weeks. I think she finally painted it back herself. I can just picture her every morning at breakfast slowly going mad looking at this bright pink wall."

In *Daughter,* everything was built as a set for the movie except the hallway and the kitchen. "It was a lot of work," says director Eduardo Rodriguez. "The production designer worked twenty-four hours a day. I don't know how long they were building those sets. They were working insane numbers of hours every day to get the stuff done in time." When you watch the film, it looks very much like a practical location.

Once you choose a location and build your sets, you will want to dress the sets to make them look as authentic as possible. The production design in *Battle of the Sexes* is pretty elaborate. An ordinary rest room is transformed before our eyes into command central. High-tech gadgetry reveals itself from the façade of ordinary bathroom décor. It looks like a lot of money was spent on doing this scene right.

"We got it all for free," reveals Eric Kripke, the film's director. "It's all donated. I was an assistant to a director on this TV movie starring Cybil Shepherd called *Journey of the Heart.* The prop master on this movie had done a Fox show called *Space: Above and Beyond.* I just made a point to work my ass off and to shake hands and to talk to everybody.

"When it came time to do *Battle of the Sexes,* which was almost two years later, I called the prop master and I said, 'Hey remember me? I'm doing this short,'" continues Kripke. "I showed him the script and asked if I could use his sci-fi props. He said, 'If you sweep out my warehouse in Sun Valley, I'll give you whatever you need for free.' Picture me shirtless, at this warehouse with rats everywhere, all day sweeping, about to collapse just to get the stuff. So we got all the stuff and then Luis Lopez, the production designer, was able to weave it all together in a really intelligent way."

ANATOMY OF A SCENE

There is a shot in *George Lucas in Love* that really sums up the whole movie. George Lucas is sitting in an empty theater, staring at the blank movie screen, searching for inspiration. Marion enters from the rear and her shadow emanates across the screen, revealing the outline of Princess Leia's famed earmuff hairstyle. George turns to see Marion enter the room, and he has found both love and inspiration.

"Dan [Shere] and I initially wrote that scene in a café, but we couldn't afford to do that," says Joe Nussbaum. "We would have to have added a day of production. We were already stretched on extras when he walks around. We couldn't try to get more extras. Extras equals friends and relatives and people we beg. So we said we need to have them meet in a place with no extras and someplace easier to shoot.

"I honestly don't know if it was Dan or me who came up with the notion of putting him in an empty theater," says Nussbaum. "And then once we came up with it, we got all excited in a geeky way. He's trying to get inspiration, he's staring at a blank screen. He goes from staring at a blank page on the typewriter to staring at a blank screen in the theater. We were all excited with the metaphor."

There was discussion at one point where someone said George should be watching a movie in the screening room. "It would have been a nightmare," says Nussbaum. "I don't even think we could have pulled it off. What movie? How do we get the rights? How do we project it? So we basically rationalized, no it's a blank screen like the blank page."

Then Nussbaum came up with the idea of the silhouette. "I'm very proud of that shot," says Nussbaum. "I think it really works well. I remember shooting it. Once we had lined it up and actually gotten it right, the flags opened and Aaron Kahn, the gaffer, said 'That is the greatest thing I've ever seen.' Aaron doesn't generally say stuff like that so it was very gratifying. That's like the image of the movie. It was the cheaper way to do it, but in retrospect, we wouldn't have been able to pull off the silhouette shot if there was an image on the screen."

ATTENTION TO DETAIL

Detail is everything when you are a director. It is all about challenging the people on your crew to do the best job they possibly can—and finding people who are capable of doing something great. "I can't take credit for all those details," admits Joe Nussbaum. "The reason the dorm room looks so fantastic is because I had a production designer who said this has got to look great. The typewriter has got to look really cool. The room has got to look intricate.

"I remember specifically telling Jennifer Darany, the hair person, we can't just fake it," says Nussbaum. "We can't just end up doing the ear-muff *Hardware Wars* joke. There are gonna be tight close-ups from the back of her head. And there are a couple over-the-shoulder shots. It has to look perfect. I don't want to see the bobby pins. I don't want to see the ar-tifice. That's what directing is all about—challenging people to get it right—not necessarily being a perfectionist, because I think I'm not a per-fectionist. I think I'm very capable of running with things when they're not perfect. But in the beginning, at least starting with the goal of perfection."

Darany created the hair pieces and showed them to Nussbaum. "There was a hair test," recalls Nussbaum. "She got together with Lisa [Jakub] and put them on. We didn't shoot it on film, but she did it. She tried it, and we knew it worked. And she tried a few different ways of how to do it before she figured it out. But that's really giving your all. That's Jennifer giving one hundred percent. She took Lisa to a wig shop and a hair place, and they worked on it and figured it out. I think that was in everything—in Eric's [Haase] lighting, in the score. Not just settling for the synth music, but really going for what makes the *Shakespeare in Love* score sound the way it does? There's this recorder. So [composer] Debbie [Lurie] got a great recorder player to come in and do it live."

The same held true for every other department. Costume design, for instance. "Give someone their marching orders as a director and say you've got to do it, you've got to nail it, you've got to get there," says Nussbaum. "Each costume has got to immediately say this is a character, but at the same time, it has to be in period. It's got to be 1967 and feel real. If Chewbacca is this big brown guy, put him in brown coveralls. And instead of his bandoleer of bullets, give him a tool belt. And then Yoda with his outfit that feels like what Yoda wears but is a sweater and pants that could be what a professor wears."

By giving your project your all, you will inspire others on your crew to do the same. At the end of *The Right Hook*, Bruno (Dave Scotti) and the angry lesbian (Keri Szymanski) get into a huge fight when he tries to pick her up at the bar. "When it came down to the fight, we wanted it to be real," says director Luke Greenfield. "We wanted it to be an ugly fight. We also agreed that it should get bigger, and bigger, and bigger. So I went back to my house and started visualizing about the most tremendous, violent images besides the bottle in the face and the typical stuff we see, like throwing someone through a glass trophy case, and things like that.

"The co-producer of *The Right Hook*, Eddie Zillian, knew a stunt coordinator, Noon Orsatti. Eddie said, 'I can get this stunt coordinator to help you.' And he came over and he had the best attitude. He came in and said, 'Let's just rock.' I said, 'What does "Let's rock" mean?' They were shooting *Fight Club* at the time. 'I'll get the guys, we'll come down and we'll kick some ass.' For free! He brought all these stunt doubles in and all this padding. We had this amazing prop master, Thomas Benton, who built these two huge break-away glass trophy cases that they crashed into."

Greenfield is very organized before he goes in to shoot a scene. "I had already shot-listed to the nth degree of exactly how I was going to shoot these fight scenes," says Greenfield. "I knew exactly how I was going to do these stunts. We had one day to do it. We were way behind. We only did the big stunt with the trophy case once. I had a chance to do it a second time, but I was too scared we were going to run out of time for the day. I should have done it again—that was my big regret."

Actors Scotti and Szymanski were real go-getters. Szymanski played the lesbian character. She had really long hair and actually chopped it all off for the role. "They went at it—pulling each other's hair, knocking each other down and kicking each other. I studied a lot of the great fights. I studied a lot of James Cameron stuff in *The Abyss* to really feel those punches hitting. I had these images in my mind of Dave taking her and throwing her over his shoulder in slow motion and smashing her through a table with this stunt double. And we actually did it. The stunt people were amazing. That was the most complicated part of the movie."

SETTING UP A SHOOTING SCHEDULE

Some people think that because their shoot is only a few days long, they do not really need to create a shooting schedule. In fact, having a shooting schedule, regardless of the length of your shoot, is always a good idea. It allows you to see on paper the logistics of each scene and will help you put together the elements you will need for each shot. Putting it down on paper allows you the perspective to arrange your time and resources in such a way that provides the maximum efficiency for shooting.

Trevor Sands shot *Inside* in three days. "Friday morning we rented a location downtown—a jail—and we shot that Steadicam shot moving down the hallway and a couple other quick pick-up shots of the guard opening the door in the beginning to take him out of the cell," says Sands. "Then we moved to the stage in Long Beach, where we had built two sets. The padded cell set we shot Friday afternoon into the evening. And all day Saturday and Sunday we shot the primary body of the film in the interview-room set. And we stayed on schedule. We didn't go too late. We tried to keep it to union hours, we paid crew members, and we had it nicely catered."

What follows is the shooting schedule for *Inside* so you can see how the script was broken down.

ONELINE SCHEDULE

Shoot Day #1 — Fri, June 15, 2001				
Scene #2pt	**INT CELL**		**DAY**	3/8 pgs.
	Orderlies pull Daniel out			
	ID: 1, 9, 10			
Scs. 3	**INT HALLWAY**		**DAY**	3/8 pgs.
	Orderlies walk Daniel, Beth, Owen, Mary, Bo down hallway			
	ID: 1, 2, 3, 4, 5, 9, 10, 12			
				Company Move
Scs. 1	**INT CELL**		**DAY**	5/8 pgs.
	Intro Daniel and his Personalities			
	ID: 1, 2, 3, 4, 5, 6, 7, 8, 13			
Scs. 2	**INT CELL**		**DAY**	3/8 pgs.
	Orderlies pull Daniel out			
	ID: 1, 9, 10			
			End Day #1 — Total Pages: 1 6/8	
Shoot Day #2 — Sat, June 16, 2001				
Scs. 4	**INT Interview Room**		**DAY**	5 5/8 pgs.
	Dr. Jane interviews Daniel, Other Dr. enters			
	ID: 1, 2, 3, 4, 5, 6, 7, 8, 11, 12, 13			
			End Day #2 — Total Pages: 5 5/8	
Shoot Day #3 — Sun, June 17, 2001				
Scs. 4	**INT Interview Room**		**DAY**	5 5/8 pgs.
	Dr. Jane interviews Daniel, Other Dr. enters			
	ID: 1, 2, 3, 4, 5, 6, 7, 8, 11, 12, 13			
			End Day #3 — Total Pages: 5 5/8	

THE LONG AND THE SHORT OF IT

Producer Steve Hein offers this parting thought on making a short film. "It's very similar to putting together a feature," says Hein. "You've got to develop a script. Raising money is still a pain in the ass. Shooting it, you still have a full camera department, a full makeup department, and full wardrobe. You have the cameras, the cranes, the trucks, the dollies, etc. You have everything you need for a feature except you're shooting in three days rather than thirty."

SHOOTING SCHEDULE

Shoot Day #1 — Fri, June 15, 2001

Scene #2pt	**INT CELL**	**DAY**	3/8 pgs.
	Orderlies pull Daniel out		

Cast Members	**Props**	**Set Dressing**
1. Daniel	keys	wall w/door
9. Orderly #1		
10. Orderly #2		

Scene #3	**INT HALLWAY**	**DAY**	3/8 pgs.
	Orderlies walk Daniel, Beth, Owen, Mary, Bo down hallway		

Cast Members	**Props**	**Special Equipment**
1. Daniel	Mary's watch	Steadicam
2. Beth		
3. Owen		
4. Mary Wright		
5. Pierce		
9. Orderly #1		

Scene #3	**INT HALLWAY**	**DAY**	3/8 pgs.
	Orderlies walk Daniel, Beth, Owen, Mary, Bo down hallway		

10. Orderly #2
12. Dr. Blake

Notes:
Dr. Jane V.O.

Company Move

Scene #1	**INT CELL**	**DAY**	5/8 pgs.
	Intro Daniel and his Personalities		

Cast Members		**Costumes**
1. Daniel		1. Daniel's inmate outfit
2. Beth		2. dirty sundress
3. Owen		3. wrinkled suit
4. Mary Wright		
5. Pierce		**Special Equiptment**
6. BO		Crane
7. Joey		
8. Harris		
13. Pops		

Scene #2	**INT CELL**	**DAY**	3/8 pgs.
	Orderlies pull Daniel out		

Cast Members	**Props**
1. Daniel	keys
9. Orderly #1	
10. Orderly #2	

END OF DAY #1 - 1 6/8 Total Pages.

SHOOTING SCHEDULE

| Scene #4 | INT Interview Room | DAY | 5 5/8 pgs. |

Dr. Jane interviews Daniel, Other Dr. enters

Cast Members	Props	Set Dressing
1. Daniel	coffee	11. white lab coat
2. Beth	Daniel's file	
3. Owen	restraints	**Special Equipment**
4. Mary Wright		Lazy Susan
5. Pierce		
6. BO		
7. Joey		
8. Harris		
11. Dr. Jane		
12. Dr. Blank		
13. Pops		

Notes:
break up scene into parts

END OF DAY #2 - 5 5/8 Total Pages.

SHOOT DAY #3 — Sun, Jun 17, 2001

| Scene #4 | INT Interview Room | DAY | 5 5/8 pgs. |

Dr. Jane interviews Daniel, Other Dr. enters

Cast Members	Props	Costumes
1. Daniel	coffee	11. white lab coat
2. Beth	Daniel's file	
3. Owen	restraints	
4. Mary Wright		
5. Pierce		
6. BO		
7. Joey		
8. Harris		
11. Dr. Jane		
12. Dr. Blake		
13. Pops		

Notes:
break up scene into parts

END OF DAY #3 - 5 5/8 Total Pages.

8

Post-Production: Everything After Wrap!

"Post-production is a very expensive part of the process of film-making, and it should be used like any other tool—to enhance the story, not to fix it or patch it. Planning as much as you can during pre-production will give you the freedom to be more creative and more productive throughout the rest of the movie-making journey."

—Eduardo Rodriguez, director

POST HASTE

The final stage of the filmmaking process is just as important as the others. After all, without post-production activities, there is no finished film. Without a finished film, you have nothing to show for all your hard work and effort, and nothing to show people what you are capable of doing as a film-maker. Do not make the most common mistake people make when producing a short film and not plan for post-production costs. Instead, anticipate your post-production needs from the very beginning and plan accordingly.

"It's always the last thing people think of . . . and the stage where most peoples' films are probably sitting," says producer Steve Hein. "They've spent all their money on production, thinking they're going to get through post on a quarter. It doesn't happen like that. Make sure you put aside some cash for post."

Post-production is a lot more than simply editing together the film. This is the time to add your visual effects; fix production sound through the looping process; add soundtrack elements including score, Foley, and other sound effects; and correct the color through telecine. In some cases, post-production might also include the transfer of the picture from the digital realm to actual film.

EDITING

They say a film is made three times: once on the page, once in production, and a third time in the cutting room. Trevor Sands was well organized from the get-go while making his short film *Inside*. He had a very clear idea of everything he wanted to do and managed to get pretty much every shot he had planned. "I edited it myself over three weeks," says Sands. "I shot three hours of footage that I cut down to eight minutes."

At the very least, you should allow one day of post-production for every day of filming. However, oftentimes with short films you are waiting for equipment to become available, waiting for a friend to have time to edit your film, editing yourself a little bit each day after you get home from work, and you are not able to function on a regular post schedule.

Sands had the luxury of time while editing *Inside*. "We shot it in May 2000. I had picture lock [the stage where editing is complete and the picture will no longer change] by the end of July," says Sands. "We were ready to mix in September. Meanwhile, I was able to work with a big lab to put together the answer print. I actually did the final mix of the piece at Soundscape with a final re-recording mixer with Jeff Jones's supervision and had it ready to go by October."

As a result of school deadlines, *Daughter* director Eduardo Rodriguez had to assemble his entire movie on a much tighter post schedule. "We had two weeks to cut the whole thing," says Rodriguez. "That was the director's cut. After that we had a week to turn it in. We had three cuts after that, and that was it. For the pre-mix we had a week. For final mix we had two weeks."

Post on *George Lucas in Love* was also incredibly short for Joe Nussbaum. "We felt we needed to have the movie done for opening weekend of [*Star Wars:*] *Episode I*— [*The Phantom Menace*]," says Nussbaum. "That was where our window of people being interested was. And that was three weeks after shooting."

Nussbaum told the editor he had a week to lock picture, and he did it. Then he gave the sound guy and the composer another week and a half. "They built all the sound," says Nussbaum. "We didn't really have to do any ADR [additional dialogue replacement]. Rick [Sanchez], our sound guy, did Foley and did effects. Debbie [Lurie] did the music and recorded it. Then we did the mix. We had a final copy on video in our hands exactly three weeks to the day from when we finished shooting."

VISUAL EFFECTS

Another misconception about short films is that because the budgets are small, they will not allow for visual effects. Sure, effects can be pricey, but that does not negate them. Like everything else, you can solicit effects houses for their help in creating your effects. You can add effects digitally right on the computer. Many physical effects can be achieved for little money and implemented at the time of filming.

Most of the visual effects for *Daughter* were actually physical effects that were mainly done on the set. This includes the blood and other makeup effects seen throughout the short. However, one big effect was put together during post.

In the final scene of the film, the little girl says, "There are no doors in hell," as her mother is locked in the bathroom and the whole set shrinks down into a small cube. That cube and others like it audibly depicting horrific acts start speeding toward a fiery image of hell. It is a fairly complex computer graphics sequence, but it looks very professional in the finished film.

Eduardo Rodriguez, the film's director, credits undergraduate student Wes Ball with pulling off the gag. "We wanted to shoot the cubes, but it was going to be too expensive to go from CGI back to film," says Rodriguez. "We knew we were going to go back to film. It wasn't going to stay on video. At the beginning there wasn't an option to do the digital stuff because we didn't have the money to do that. So we always thought that we were going to make these tiny cubes, put them on the sound stage, light each one of them individually, and try to just dolly back from the cubes." The accompanying soundtrack would give the impression that each cube contained an act as horrible as the mother who killed her own daughter.

They started building the cubes, but it was extremely difficult to make them look good. "They were solid cubes like something you would do at school in a kindergarten project," explains Rodriguez. "It started getting tougher and tougher. We wanted to buy plastic cubes, but they were so expensive that it wasn't going to be an option, either. They only came in three standard sizes so we weren't going to be able to have the depth of field we wanted."

The school got wind of Rodriguez's production problems and told him to explore the costs associated with transferring digital images to film. They told the filmmaker if it was possible, they would give him some extra money to do it.

Producer Jim Sims found a facility at Georgia State University that has the ability to transfer video from the computer back to film. "It was another university that was very helpful," says Rodriguez. "They said, 'Not a problem. We'll do it. The only thing that it's gonna cost you is the film for the transfer and the processing. We're not gonna charge you anything else.'" At the end of the day, it cost Rodriguez a mere $200 to do the whole thing.

Now that they knew how they were going to tackle this post-production problem, they needed to find someone who could do it correctly. "We went to the computer school and one of the professors there said, 'I can do it for you guys. Not a problem,'" says Rodriguez. "I don't know if it was a communication problem, or what it was, but we never got the right thing with him. It was very tough going over and over trying to explain what we wanted. Every time he gave us something, it was completely different than what we had imagined."

Time was not on their side. "We were getting close to the very end of the movie," says Rodriguez. "We were very worried about what was going to happen with the cubes, because without that shot it would be very hard to finish the movie the way we wanted. During that time, everyone came to me and asked me how I was doing. And I said, 'I'm really not doing too well because I've got this serious problem with the cubes.'"

The good thing about complaining to everyone is that one day Rodriguez complained to a student named Wes Ball. Ball, who had extensive experience with CGI, offered to help the director with his problem. "I told him, 'If you can help me out, that would be awesome because I don't know what to do.'"

Ball figured out the problem and came up with a solution to the director's satisfaction. "I have to say that Wes Ball is a genius," says Rodriguez. "He knew how to do the whole thing. And actually the fiery horizon in the back, which I thought was a great idea, came from him. It helped a lot to make people understand that idea of hell. Originally it was only going to be the cubes. And Ball asked, 'What if we put this fire here?' It looked awesome. So Wes Ball was a salvation man who came to rescue us from that big nightmare and that big hell that was the cube thing."

SOUND

Sound is another integral factor to any film. This includes not only the production sound, but sound effects, soundtrack songs, score, Foley, and ADR, when necessary. Creating a great mix is an art unto itself. Align yourself with the best people to create the right sound for your short film.

In the short film *Inside,* Jeremy Sisto plays a young man with multiple personality disorder. Inside his head, he hears the voices of various characters pulling him in several different directions. These voices speak to him randomly, often more than one at the same time. He has a total of about ten different voices in his head. Because of the very structure of the film, sound design was an integral part to pulling off this short.

Director Trevor Sands initially cut some pre-mixes in the Avid, essentially knowing where offscreen dialogue would go. "I was then able to put the entire movie together in the Avid with temp music and a temp dialogue track mix," says Sands. "I then gave that to the composer and sound designer, Jeffrey Allen Jones. He did both, which is why he was ideal for the project."

Jones had all his own equipment, including his own Pro Tools setup. "He's not only a talented composer, but he's also a talented sound editor, dialogue editor, FX editor, and mixer," says Sands. "He did *The Shark Tank Redemption,* which Gary Bryman produced. When I was looking into composers and sound designers, Gary hooked me up with Jeff.

"It turned out that Jeff had the best type of music for what I wanted to do, which was more of an ambient, low-key score," says Sands. "He also happened to have the added bonus of all the equipment and the experience as a sound designer. And it seemed like the ideal project for him to show off his stuff because the nature of the project was almost like the sound design was part of the music.

"I pitched it to him as an opportunity to merge sound design with score in a way that is rarely done and try to use the different voices of these characters as instruments in a score," continues Sands. "He had all the separate tracks of all the dialogue lined up and spent a long time and a lot of work putting it together. I'm very appreciative of his efforts because he did a fantastic job."

Eduardo Rodriguez's film *Daughter* also relied heavily on sound design. "Horror movies are fifty percent sound and fifty percent images," says Rodriguez. "It's very important in a horror movie to have strong images, and sound design is very important to me because I think that's what makes a horror movie a good horror movie."

Rodriguez wanted the sound in *Daughter* to be as good as any professional movie he had ever seen. "I owe that to Jason Lang," says Rodriguez. "He was the sound designer for my previous movie, another short film we did in Tallahassee called *Symbiosis.* The sound design for that movie was so good that it got selected for the Vernow Award at the Sound Designers Guild of America in the short film category. That was the only one that was live-action. The other ones were all computer graphics. Ours was the only one with real people. So Lang was so good I asked him if he wanted to do the sound design for my thesis and he said, 'Yes, of course.' We work together very well."

MUSIC

Most people do not realize how expensive it is to put music into a film. Just because you are making a low-budget short does not necessarily mean you will get a break on costs. In fact, some music might be unattainable. Try getting the rights to use the new Madonna single in your film. Good luck. Companies like ASCAP (American Society of Composers, Authors, and Publishers), which control the publishing rights to songs, are willing to work with young filmmakers, but be careful. If you want to use a song, there are several different rights attached to it, including the right to reproduce the music and the rights to the original recording.

"Make sure you get clearances for your music," advises Steve Hein. You have to get the rights to use the song, and you have to get the rights to use the recording. That's why it's often easier to just compose an original score or original songs specifically for the film.

Sometimes you will be allowed to use recordings of popular songs in your movie for a nominal fee or no charge at all, but generally there are restrictions that come with that privilege. Most commonly, exhibition of the finished short would be limited to film festivals. If a sale of the film resulted from a festival screening, the filmmaker would have to pay premium rates if he wanted the song to remain in the film.

Bryan Gordon pulled a major coup in getting permission for the classic songs he uses in *Ray's Male Heterosexual Dance Hall*. "We pleaded and begged and told them it would be used for festivals most of the time," says Gordon. "There's usually festival rights, which are a lot less than you would have to pay if you actually got distributed. The problem is, if it does go to festivals, there's now a market for short films on different networks and for distribution around the world, so you will have to have the right cleared, or clearable. That costs quite a bit if you're using a very popular song. So you've got to check out all that stuff first."

TRANSFER

If you shoot your short digitally but you plan to hit the festival circuit, you will need to transfer to film. Likewise, if you shoot on film but want to distribute on video, you will need to transfer to tape. In either case, transfer costs might end up being high. Be sure to plan these expenses into your budget from the very beginning.

Although Joe Nussbaum shot *George Lucas in Love* on 35mm film, initially he did not make a film print of the movie. Instead, he output the film to video for street team distribution. "In retrospect, we wish we would have made a print," says Nussbaum. "We loved how our video came out looking. We went back and cut negative long after all the hubbub."

The video master was on digi-Beta, and Nussbaum made lots of copies on VHS and sent it all around Los Angeles. "There was a lot of hoopla," says Nussbaum. "It was incredible. Then we started getting into festivals. And then we went back and cut our negative and made a film print, which was expensive and a pain because there were a lot of wipes and opticals and the credits were weird. If we had to do it today, we definitely would have taken that digi-Beta and transferred it to film. It definitely would have been cheaper, and I actually think it would have looked great."

PICK-UPS

Every once in a while you have the luxury of doing some re-shoots, or additional photography. You assemble the movie as best you can, and then you realize there is still something missing or not working that cannot be fixed with the existing footage. Although a costly proposition to undertake, there is always the option of shooting more film.

"There's a scene in *Daughter* that was cut," says Eduardo Rodriguez. "When she gets to the bathtub and she opens the curtains, there was a bracelet—the thing that she grabs when she wakes up the first time. The bracelet with the cross was on the bottom of the bathtub, which was filled with water. She reaches for it and then a rain of dolls, like the dolls that the little girl is holding, start falling from the ceiling. They're all bloody and all messed up. After that is when the little girl comes into the room and tells her what is going on.

"It didn't look as good as I thought it would," says Rodriguez. "It looked a little bit comedic. It looked like people were throwing dolls from above the stage, which actually was what was happening. So it didn't have the effect I wanted it to have, which was the rain of pain or rain of all the wrong things she did."

Because that scene was cut out of the film, Rodriguez had to shoot a couple more shots to make the transition a little bit smoother between opening the curtain and going to where the little girl was. "We shot a couple inserts and pick-ups," says Rodriguez. "There were some shots that had some flash, and we tried to fix that. I don't think we shot any major stuff in pick-ups, just fixed a couple things we had."

THE MORAL: PLAN FOR POST

The most important advice you can gain from this chapter is to budget for post-production from the very beginning. The most common mistake filmmakers make is not allocating enough resources to finish their movie. They shoot the film, it is in the can, and they might even have people waiting to see it, but they have run out of money and are not able to complete the movie. Do not let this happen to you.

9

Marketing: Coming Soon to a Theater Near You

"The more you get your film out there and get people to see it and create a buzz about it, the better off you're going to be—no matter what position you're in."

—Eric Haase, producer and cinematographer

IF AT FIRST YOU DON'T SUCCEED . . .

Eric Kripke finished making *Truly Committed* right after he graduated from USC. In the meantime, he was writing a script that tonally was very similar to the short film. He was hoping to get the short into various film festivals so he might get scouted by agents or studio executives. He also sent out the short and the script to agents to see if he could find representation.

"It didn't really work out," says Kripke. "I collected huge stacks of rejection notices from agents. Everyone liked the movie but couldn't really do anything with it. It didn't get into Sundance, although it did get into some other film festivals and did really well."

Over the next two years, Kripke begged his parents for cash. He worked odd jobs to pay the bills. Not wanting to put his film school education to waste, he shot industrial videos for organizations like the United Jewish Federation. He also did odd jobs around the industry to gain experience, such as interning for the director of a TV movie starring Cybil Shepherd.

A lot of Kripke's friends took jobs working in development, but he didn't feel that was the most productive route for him. "I'm of the opinion that if you want to be a writer-director, you probably shouldn't work in development," says Kripke. "You have to have friends who are in development or know people that you can show your scripts to, But that work is so hard and exhausting that to be able to work that job *and* create the material that will be able to take you out of that job becomes really difficult. You need to have a job like actors do, where you can write all day and you're a waiter at night."

Once Kripke resolved that *Truly Committed* was not the calling card he hoped it would be, he decided to try again with a new short. "I approached Gary [Bryman] and Steve [Hein] and said, 'Instead of paying off our *Truly Committed* loan, let's shoot.' And I love that attitude. That's the attitude you need. Whatever it takes to get something on film, do it. So we took the money, and we pulled together *Battle of the Sexes*."

In *Battle of the Sexes*, Kripke finally had a totally effective marketing tool. Things came together very quickly. He got an agent off the strength of the film. But he had been so burned out on the festival circuit with *Truly Committed* that he shied away from sending this one out at all. "I was sort of over it," admits Kripke. "I didn't want to travel around. It didn't really help that much with *Truly Committed*. I was sick of going to the post office!"

However, Kripke did apply to the mother of all festivals, Sundance. And just for fun, he also entered *Truly Committed* into Park City's other big film festival, Slamdance, even though that film had been rejected by Sundance the previous year. Then the strangest thing happened. Both films got into their respective festivals. What's more, Kripke found himself with a great marketing hook to promote himself as a filmmaker.

"I had two films playing across the street from each other," says Kripke. "At that point, I was the only short filmmaker to have done that.

That year, the only other people who had done that were the *South Park* guys with features at each festival. And I was the guy with shorts at each festival. So going into Sundance, there was a little window where there's a mention about it in the trades. You could slide it into conversations with the people in the various audiences. It was sort of a unique thing."

If that was not enough, Kripke continued to generate buzz when *Truly Committed* won the Audience Award at Slamdance. "It kind of kept going," says Kripke. "Fate opened up this window. A lot of people were giving me their cards. Going back to Los Angeles after that, you have about two or three weeks where you're still in people's heads."

Kripke had planned ahead. He had written a feature-length screenplay based on *Battle of the Sexes*. As soon as he returned from Sundance and Slamdance, his agent sent out the script to capitalize on the festival buzz. "It's not a bad idea to have a feature version of your short film," advises Kripke. "It's a good idea because they'll see the film, especially if it's a really good film they'll get it. If you have a feature script, that's a great next step in your strategizing."

MARKETING

Hollywood is an industry that incorporates marketing in every facet of the business. This starts long before and goes way beyond the theatrical release of a film. On a daily basis, filmmakers must convince executives to read a script, persuade financiers to fund movies, and encourage actors to attach themselves to projects. Simply put, they must impel others to take a chance on them. This can be achieved through the filmmakers' energy, enthusiasm, and passion.

The same holds true for short filmmakers during the process of making a short and while using the short itself as an effective marketing tool. But remember, it is only a tool—one piece of the puzzle. You still need a marketing plan to complement your short film.

You must be able to sell yourself in a room. Giving a good meeting is as important as making a great movie. If you are too shy or unable to express yourself during a Hollywood lunch, problems will arise. Enter each meeting with an agenda, and effectively deliver your message.

You need to convince an agent or manager to take a stake in your career. With all the filmmakers out there, why should they represent you? You need to sell them on that notion. Convince them why you are the best client for them. Let them prove that they are the best agent for you. Marketing can work both ways.

Ideally, a studio executive will watch your short and bring you in to meet about a specific project. He wants to hear about your creative vision for the studio's film. What are your ideas? What unique abilities can you bring to the project? Show them that you are the best person for the job.

Not a day goes by that I don't employ some form of marketing in my job. In fact, no one in Hollywood can be successful without implementing these skills into their daily routine. Savvy marketing techniques are the skills that will help move your Hollywood career forward. An understanding of basic marketing principals is essential for filmmakers. A few we will talk about in depth in this chapter include generating a word-of-mouth "buzz" for your project, taking advantage of all opportunities that come your way, and leveraging those opportunities into career-making success.

WORD OF MOUTH

The best way to generate publicity is through good, old-fashioned word of mouth. You see a movie you enjoy. You probably recommend it to your friends. They tell some of their friends. Before you know it, you have created your own buzz, and everybody in town wants to see the film.

Hollywood works very much the same way. People talk to each other, telling them about this great short film they saw or an amazing new filmmaker they discovered. There is a great sense of pride involved with the discovery of new talent. As a new filmmaker, you can use this to your advantage.

When Luke Greenfield screened his student project coming out of USC, he canvassed the town to get the industry into the theater seats. "I did so much work, inviting the world and calling every assistant of every agent and every assistant of every creative executive," says Greenfield, who did manage to get an agent out of it. "I signed at ICM a couple days later, and I thought I had it made."

Sending invitations to a screening is a good idea, but be careful not to cross the line. "Don't send your film directly to studios unsolicited because they won't watch it," warns Steve Hein. "I find that everybody knows somebody who knows somebody, no matter where you live. Get it to them. My feeling on it is that the cream always rises to the top. If it's a really good film, it will have its legs and it will take on a life of its own. It will get out there."

People will spread the word when they find something they like. "Our favorite things to do when we have a new film is to make one hundred dubs, give them to four or five assistants we know around town, and tell them to send it to all their friends," says Hein "They all want to feel like they have a sense of ownership of the film, like they discovered this guy. Then they show it to their bosses, and the next thing you know you have this built-in underground buzz about it."

BE READY WHEN OPPORTUNITY KNOCKS

Luke Greenfield's intention was to be ready when opportunity knocked. "My whole goal was to have *The Right Hook* and to have a feature film script ready to go," says Greenfield. "I could show them the short, see that they love that, then show them the feature script. We call it the one-two punch. The problem was that I was not a good enough writer to really write the feature-length script."

If you are a struggling filmmaker who clearly is not a writer, you can choose one of the following options: Option a piece of material from a writer that you can then direct; partner with a writer and create something together that you can then direct; struggle writing until you finally pull it off; or give up trying. Ideally, you will choose one of the first two options.

"I was suffering. I was struggling. I didn't have time," admits Greenfield. "The feature I wanted to do was a comedy. *The Right Hook* captured my comedic sense. But people started seeing rough cuts of *The Right Hook* and it started taking off real fast." Greenfield was not even close to being done with his feature-length script when word of mouth on his short exploded. Without his next project ready to go, would Greenfield's marketing plan go to waste? As you shall see in Chapter Eleven: *Landing the Deal,* this story has an ending you would only find in a movie.

CRITICAL RECOGNITION

A surefire way to draw attention to your film is by winning an award or getting fantastic reviews. This acclaim can then form the basis of your marketing campaign. "You've got to see this short. It just won first place in the Cannes Film Festival." "This short film is a must-see. Kevin Thomas of the *LA Times* gave it a rave review." "Did you see the five movies that were nominated for best documentary short for this year's Oscar race?"

Oh yes, the Oscars. The pinnacle of success in Hollywood. But does being nominated for an Oscar, or even winning one, guarantee a successful feature career for a short filmmaker?

Jana Sue Memel has been nominated eleven times for shorts she has produced. Three of those nominations turned into wins. "Winning, if it's not a drama, will get you a zillion meetings," says Memel. "Whether it actually gets you a movie or not depends on you. If your short was a drama, you'll get some meetings, but unless you have a script to put forward, nobody is going to stand in line to offer you your next drama.

"All studio dramas are star-driven and you have to be able as a director to attract stars to get the film made. There's always a tiny little flurry of interest after the Oscars and then it generally dissipates unless you have something everybody wants. Like everything else in Hollywood, it depends on who you are and how you handle your fame."

According to Memel, having an Oscar gives you more to brag about. "You have a leg up on somebody else who is as good as you are." Everything else being equal, an Oscar-nominated or Oscar-winning short might just give you the push you need to convince someone to give you that shot to direct a feature.

Bryan Gordon won an Oscar for directing the short film *Ray's Male Heterosexual Dance Hall,* which, incidentally, Jana Sue Memel produced. "In some ways, winning the Oscar has always been a good thing for me," says Gordon. "At the time, I was developing screenplays and writing screenplays and wanting to get my own screenplay off the ground. Having the Oscar was a real help. In fact, it did help get the initial financing for my film."

When Gordon won his Oscar, there was a great deal of "heat" around Hollywood about him for a couple years. "There is a window of time where people are asking, 'When is he going to do a big feature?'" says Gordon. "I didn't make a feature of my own until 1995: *Pie in the Sky* with Josh Charles and Ann Heche. Then I went off and did a John Hughes movie called *Career Opportunities* with Jennifer Connolly." But to this day, the short continues to open doors.

"From my vantage point, people always tell me it's been one of their favorite all-time short films," says Gordon. "It plays at various venues all the time around the world. It's always an example of my creativity, and I would say it is my favorite piece of work I have done because I was able to be who I was. In filmmaking, you rarely get a chance to be the auteur." The film has also opened many doors in television. Gordon has spent the last five years continually directing TV, from *Ally McBeal* to *The West Wing.*

Peter Lord has been nominated for three Oscars and won one in the short animated film category. For him, it definitely was a changing point in his career. "I had no idea you could be nominated for a short film," says Lord. "Getting nominated was fantastic. Going to the Oscars was fantastic. That was such a great experience.

AND THE NOMINEES ARE . . .

Jana Sue Memel belongs to the shorts branch of the Academy of Motion Pictures, Arts, and Sciences. "It used to be mostly composed of animators who were slightly older than other filmmakers," says Memel. "That branch is changing in its composition. Access to filmmaking equipment has now become quite easy. So these days the quality of films that come to the branch from around the world is staggering."

There is a process to being eligible for nomination. You must screen your short for three days in a theater in Los Angeles and/or New York for paid admission twice a day or it has to have been at an approved film festival. Then there is a screening committee of twenty-five to thirty members. They ask as many people in the branch as possible to show up. "It's really a lot of work," says Memel. "The screening committee watches every film submitted and gets them down to the ten. The whole branch is invited to watch the ten. They must come to the screening venue to watch them. You're not allowed to vote on films you haven't seen. They screen them in Los Angeles, New York, London, and San Francisco. Those ten are then narrowed to five. Then there's two or three screenings to which the whole membership is invited."

Memel has seen a wide range of movies in those ten. "It's really about those peoples' personal preference and tastes," says Memel. "People have asked me for years, 'What's the trick?' The trick is to make a movie. There is no rhyme or reason as to what they pick, which I think is true of all people who appraise art."

In 2002, the branch received 102 submissions. In 2001, they received 149. "It's not about politics," says Memel. "They literally sit there and watch the movies. People who work in the shorts branch screening committee put in sixty to eighty hours, and they're doing it for no money. They're doing it because they care."

"It was so funny when we went because the studio was about eight to ten people—quite a small team," says Lord. "We weren't very well off. All our tuxedos came from the thrift shop. Our life was very quiet and normal and very far from Hollywood. We never met anyone from the film business. We just quietly got on with what we were doing, very successfully.

"Then, suddenly, you're in Hollywood amongst this outrageous opulence and display, rubbing shoulders with people you had only seen on the screen before," says Lord. "It was like a fantasy, but a very enjoyable one. When we won, that was big news in Britain because not very many Oscars are won in Britain. If there aren't any Michael Caines winning Oscars, then the media pays a lot of attention to whoever does. In that case, it was us."

With the excitement of an Oscar win, Lord's animation company, Aardman Studios, was able to grow and expand. It provided valuable opportunities to continue to do more shorts. It also provided the cache and opened doors to the world of feature films.

COMING SOON

In Hollywood, marketing and distribution go hand in hand. Many studios house these departments under the same roof because they are closely related. The same holds true for short films. As such, the following chapter on distribution will tie in closely to what you have just read.

10

Distribution: Getting Your Film to the Right People

"The number one thing that filmmakers want is exhibition because they know that people are out there looking for the next big thing."

—Susan Peterson, vice president, distribution, Hypnotic Films

RELEASE

In film school, students screen their short films in the classroom so they can receive feedback on their work from their peers. This constructive criticism helps a filmmaker to grow and evolve, and it's a chance to get unbiased opinions of what worked and what did not work in their movies.

In addition, a screening serves as an opportunity to entertain an audience with original work. There is an indescribable feeling of satisfaction you get when you witness an audience laugh at the right joke or scream at the right scare. This is why we make movies.

Today there are thousands of short films being made every year. Many of these shorts are done outside the academic setting. Several distribution outlets have been created to show audiences the fruits of all this hard labor as a result of the volume of product available.

In the early days of cinema, shorts were screened in movie houses before the feature presentation. We see that happen occasionally today, but it is no longer a common practice. That said, there are many other methods of distribution that capitalize on showing short films. Now more than ever, shorts of all types are readily available for mass consumption through the Internet, VHS and DVD, on cable, and elsewhere.

READY FOR DISTRIBUTION

Different distribution outlets prefer that short films be in specific formats. Susan Peterson is the vice president of distribution at Hypnotic Films. She sells short-form programming to various outlets, including cable and foreign television. "Unless someone is looking for student films, indie, or cutting-edge films, format does matter," says Peterson. "Among the distribution group, we prefer 16mm and 35mm over DV. That is for distribution reasons. If it's shot on DV, we won't be able to tell that. That's not to say that there's not a place for those types of films; we just tend to work with the best of the best channels who want the best of the best, and they tend to want those types of formats."

At IFilm, an Internet distribution outlet, format is not as big a concern. "It doesn't matter what they shot it in," claims IFilm executive vice president Adam Stein. "If it's film stock, they're going to have to transfer it from some mechanism that we can then encode from. If they're shooting in 35mm, they're probably interested in filmmaking as a profession and they're doing that for the purposes of having the experience of shooting in 35mm, and also the ability to demonstrate that to potential buyers. On the Internet, it really doesn't matter. For the quality of the image on a computer screen, you can't really discern the difference between something that's shot on 35mm and something that's shot on DV because the pixels are all condensed into a very small screen size."

For Internet distribution, films have to be converted to digital files. "It does not matter what the format is," says Stein. "We are technology agnostic in that we allow our audience to watch the content in a variety of different formats—Windows Media Player, RealNetworks, QuickTime—so we don't have a preference of the type of player. Then we encode in a variety of different speeds so if you're at home watching on a dial-up, we stream to that setting, or if you're at work on a T1, we encode it at a higher bit rate. Filmmakers can submit on a variety of formats. They can submit it on a VHS tape, they can ftp a file to us, or they can give us an Mpeg file."

SELF-DISTRIBUTION

Self-distribution is not the most productive method to release your film to the masses. However, it might possibly be the best way to target a specific audience set, such as film industry executives or agents and managers. This is why Joe Nussbaum initially chose self-distribution for his short *George Lucas in Love*.

"How can we become that tape that everybody wants to see?" asked Nussbaum. "How can we become *Troops*? We made 300 copies. We were very ambitious. And we just started getting them to people. Joseph [Levy] got it to all sorts of contacts he had at the William Morris Agency where he had worked and to producers he knew. Everyone he could think of—agents, managers, producers, development people. [Executive producer] Gary Bryman took a handful of copies. One of the people he gave it to right away was [manager] J. C. Spink, who had actually gone out with *Saving Ryan's Privates* and *Herd* (Mike Mitchell's film). Spink and [partner] Chris Bender wanted to sign me right away, and they did. The thing is, if people really like it, then it can happen really quickly, and it can snowball."

Most people self-distribute on VHS, but some ambitious young filmmakers burn their shorts onto DVD. This is what Trevor Sands decided to do with his short *Inside*. In addition to the slick packaging we are accustomed to seeing on most feature-length DVDs, Sands also included all the standard extras such as director commentary, a making of documentary, and a gag reel.

"The DVD was a very smart choice because it really presents the film in a package that people respond to instead of your standard dubbed VHS tape with white label and black text, which is what everybody gets," explains Sands. "By having these classy final product pieces of work, it's showing that you have the forethought and creative drive to come up with an entire movie. The only difference between this and your standard studio feature is that this is only eight minutes long. I think it was fairly effective in terms of making people sit down and watch it as opposed to just popping it in and playing it while they're making phone calls."

In addition to self-distribution on VHS and DVD, there are a few companies that buy and sell shorts to consumers in these formats. One such company is Apollo Cinema, which ultimately bought *George Lucas in Love* to distribute on a short film collection. In fact, it's available for purchase in stores and online. "It outsold [*Star Wars: Episode I—The*] *Phantom Menace* in its first week on Yahoo!" says Gary Bryman.

INTERNET

More than any other distribution outlet, the Internet has provided the greatest opportunities for short filmmakers. With websites like AtomFilms and IFilm, shorts have become instantly accessible to film fans around the globe. With little to no cost to filmmakers, these sites post shorts online that anyone with a computer can access. Filmmakers receive feedback from those who watch their movies. In many cases, this is how young filmmakers have been discovered by Hollywood.

A few years ago, a creative executive at an advertising agency in Chicago was surfing the Internet when he discovered *Battle of the Sexes* playing on IFilm. He watched the short and apparently liked what he saw. That same day he had a meeting in which Anheuser-Busch was looking for a Bud Light commercial that might appeal to women. The executive pitched Eric Kripke's film as the new campaign. They loved the idea!

"They didn't know who I was, but they tracked me down," says

Kripke, who was very excited by the prospect of turning his short into an advertising campaign. "I walked away with a huge commercial directing opportunity for no other reason at all except some dude was cruising the Internet and came across my film."

A month later, Kripke was on set. "I was able to bring in the same actor, the male lead, into the commercial," says Kripke. "That morning, I was getting ready and he was getting ready and we both ended up at the craft service table where the chef with the white hat is by the omelet bar busting out omelets for us. And we turned to each other and caught each other's eyes and started laughing our asses off because it was like, 'Remember the last shoot where it was a box of Wheaties?' That was a really fun experience."

IFilm
www.ifilm.com

IFilm was started in 1999 by Luke McDonough and Roger Raderman just prior to the Internet boom. McDonough and Raderman saw a need for providing an outlet of short films to people who were using the Internet for entertainment purposes. They were big fans of the entertainment industry, and they had a wealth of knowledge in Internet technologies. They joined forces with Kevin Wendle, one of the original founders of the Fox Broadcasting Network, and soon IFilm became a massive aggregation center for all short films on the web.

"The original concept was to provide a place for filmmakers to get their product and content viewed by the public," says Adam Stein, executive vice president of IFilm. "I'm responsible for everything from sales and marketing, business development, to overseeing content, and all strategies for the growth of IFilm.com.

"IFilm was always built on the notion of being filmmaker friendly and allowing filmmakers to retain the rights to their work," says Stein. "When the Internet first launched, there was a very big and fast-moving desire by a lot of companies to own the short film and short form entertainment space. They were going to do it by acquiring content, paying for content, then hoping that the audience would follow once you actually had the content."

IFilm took a very different stance. "IFilm's tact was, we're not going to buy your piece of content," explains Stein. "We're not going to make it our business model to pay for the acquisition of content. What we're going to do is ask you to give us the Internet rights to distribute your content. They're going to be nonexclusive rights to allow you to go ahead and potentially sell that product to a studio, for example, or a DVD manufacturer who might actually want to monetize that product. We really believe that we are a platform to allow filmmakers to exhibit their product, and our strategy is that we build the audience first and if we built the audience, filmmakers would come to us.

"We clearly have the largest selection of short films online—tens of thousands of short films," says Stein. "We have great, deep relationships with filmmakers who continue to give us their product for distribution. But at the end of the day they get to retain their rights and we're not taking advantage of them and paying a minimal amount of money and reaping the rewards."

IFilm's submission policy is easy. Filmmakers can go to the main website and electronically submit their content. There is a form that allows them to deliver the content and explain who they are as a filmmaker. The content is then reviewed. Filmmakers can also make submissions through the mail.

IFilm also has a team of scouts. "We have a team that is responsible for scouring the landscape and finding those nuggets and gems," says Stein. "We have people who go to film markets and film festivals. We have people on staff who have relationships with film schools across the country. We really do take a very proactive approach in trying to develop relationships with filmmakers across the country who might not necessarily be at a major institution but at a smaller university, for example, producing content."

The site gets a tremendous amount of content. "We have an editorial staff that watches every piece of content that comes into the building," says

Stein. "They use a set of criteria to determine whether or not a piece of content is deemed to have great appeal. It doesn't necessarily have to have mass appeal; it could be something that is so dynamic and so unique that although we think the consumption side of that audience might be minimal, it's just a piece of work that's so brilliant that we have to keep it up there. They use this set of criteria to help them decide what to put up on the site."

IFilm has had its share of Hollywood success stories. In addition to Eric Kripke, other emerging filmmakers have been discovered by showing their short film online. Jonathan Liebersman, the director of *Darkness Falls,* started with a short on IFilm. "Jonathan had a movie that came out on IFilm called *Genesis and Catastrophe,*" says Stein. "He clearly would attribute the successes he had at IFilm for helping him launch his career. We did an interview with him in which he talked about how he had his short film on IFilm and it allowed him to have a calling card to go out there and get seen by a lot of Hollywood executives. Initially he tried to submit his work to Sundance and the Toronto Film Festival, but he wasn't successful so he came to IFilm to get his product distributed, and lo and behold, he wound up parlaying that into a very successful career."

Hypnotic
www.hypnotic.com

The idea for Hypnotic Films was conceived by Jeremy Bernard about three years ago as an online destination for the independent filmmaking community for short films. It was launched as reelshort.com, and like many websites at the time, it was a place for this community to come and watch their work online and get it out there for people to see. The website soon merged with Nibblebox, which was headed by director Doug Lyman and executive Dave Bartis. Then Universal Pictures became interested in the company and invested in it. At that time, the name changed to Hypnotic Films, and the business model also changed to become more of a traditional entertainment studio than solely an online destination.

"The whole mission of Hypnotic was to find this untapped filmmaking talent from around the globe, sort of the next big filmmakers you will hear about for the next ten years," says Susan Peterson, vice president of distribution. "In a sense, Universal looks to us, as they had other companies, as a farm team to find the next big up-and-coming talent. We help them not only through distributing their short films, which is what I do, but also by getting them involved in development of series, features, commercials, and branded entertainment."

One way Hypnotic has been successful at identifying filmmaking talent is through their Million Dollar Film Festival. Filmmakers submit a short that they have directed to enter into the contest. The best shorts are chosen, and those filmmakers are then given an assignment to direct another short. The two shorts are then judged together to see a broader spectrum of what the filmmakers are capable of. The winner of the contest receives one million dollars to direct a film.

Jeff Wadlow, a graduate of the USC Peter Stark program, was a recent winner of the Million Dollar Film Festival. His short film was called *The Tower of Babble*. "He made a very good short film," says Gene Klein, Hypnotic's vice president of acquisitions. "It was one that certainly caught our attention when we were reviewing all the submissions. He had some industry connections because he had also worked as an actor, and he's aggressive, and he had gone through the Stark program. Because he had the means to meet people, his short film got into many of the right hands. People were interested and yet nobody wanted to sign him. He wasn't making that next step by virtue of the short film."

Then Wadlow made an extreme film, which is the portion of the Million Dollar Film Festival where he was given ten days to make a digital short. "It was extremely accomplished, especially since it was done within ten days from beginning of casting to the screening," explains Klein. "When he came back from that phase of our competition, we started sending that film around with his first short. He was signed by William Morris, and he started getting meetings at production companies for other projects both as a writer and as a director for hire. What allowed him to break through the clutter was consistency. He had an accomplished short film that got some peoples' attention, but then when they saw the second one and they saw that it was accomplished on a limited period of time with limited resources, they knew this guy is clearly going to be a winner."

Klein cites Wadlow's distinct point of view as the reason the young filmmaker advanced to the next round of the competition. "When you watched his short film, you really felt like you were sinking into a world," says Klein. "And he happened to have a gimmick in his short. Some gimmicks work; some don't. This one happened to work. This was several interwoven stories that use the same dialogue under very different circumstances. And that's where the title comes from—*Tower of Babble*—how words can mean very different things under different circumstances. It had very good execution and a very good series of stories, but it also had a very good big idea—a message that it wanted people to come across with. And he executed well on all levels."

Wadlow is currently hard at work rewriting a script that he plans to direct as part of his prize for winning the contest. It is a modern reinterpretation of *The Boy Who Cried Wolf*. "He picked a feature idea to present to us where there was a line between the work he did in his shorts and what he wanted to do as a feature," says Klein. "The line in this case was that he took a relatively simple, concise idea and executed it very well."

Another success story from Hypnotic is a television show called *Delusions*. The show is based on a short film called *Delusions in Modern Primitivism* by Dan Loflin about a man who realizes he is the world's biggest jerk so he moves from New York to Alabama to figure out where he went wrong. After Hypnotic acquired the short film for distribution, they helped the young filmmaker develop the series idea and then shopped it to studios. FX Networks bought the show, and Warner Bros. Television will produce it with Hypnotic Films.

Hypnotic has also been successful in the branded entertainment division. When *Terry Tate: Office Linebacker* was originally submitted to Hypnotic, the overall quality of the short was not that great. "But the writing style behind it, the character in it, and the sensibility of it was just tremendously hilarious," says Peterson. "The branded entertainment folks went around to the places where they had relationships to have them look at the film as a character to develop in commercials."

Reebok ultimately commissioned Hypnotic to come up with commercials using the character from the film. "We bumped up the quality and fleshed it out a little bit," says Peterson. "The character and the filmmaker are both going to continue to be part of that entire process."

Hypnotic finds short films at film festivals. They track well over one hundred festivals and attend a subset of those. They have also developed associations with film schools that have consistently churned out filmmakers who are at the top of their game. Some of these institutions include AFI, USC, NYU, and Columbia University. They also get a lot of submissions off their website. "The website helps us maintain a presence," says Klein. "The website allows people to read about us and deliver our message, but we still have to reach out to people a lot."

For filmmakers interested in submitting their short to Hypnotic, they simply go to the main website and click on the "Filmmakers" button for instructions on where to send their short film. "The great thing about our company is the short film is just the beginning of their relationship with us," says Klein. "We do acquire shorts, and we do distribute shorts, but we're very much a traditional film and television company."

Producers Steve Hein and Gary Bryman also have a partnership with Hypnotic in which they function as their sister management company representing some of the filmmakers they scout at film festivals. They also function as their in-house production company for their short films and branded entertainment campaigns.

AtomFilms
www.atomfilms.com

AtomFilms was started in June 1998, and the original website was launched in November of that same year. It began as a business-to-business site. The consumer website was not launched until March 1999. In January 2001, the Seattle-based AtomFilms merged with Shockwave and relocated to San Francisco.

Company founder and CEO Mika Salmi had the idea back in 1992. "The original idea was a cable channel," says Salmi. "It evolved in 1994 to a CD-ROM business. Then after I was working at Real Networks for a couple years, I thought maybe it would be an Internet business. When I actually launched it, I wasn't sure anybody would fund it, so the original business plan for Atom was to try and license the world's best short form content, both animations and films and then resell those licenses, or distribute them to other companies that would pay for that usage. So it wasn't originally to be a consumer website as much as it was to try and make money, be a kind of library, be an aggregator of the best, and then sell them to other places."

In the early days, AtomFilms sold their product to cable TV, international television, airlines, hotels, and other websites that needed content like Go, the Disney/Infoseek portal, and Snap from NBCi. Very quickly they launched their consumer site because they realized people actually wanted to watch movies on the Internet. So the company broadened its business model to also be consumer focused, and centered around having advertising on the website. For a period of time AtomFilms also sold VHS tapes and DVDs directly to consumers.

"We were a little bit different than a lot of the other Hollywood sites," says Salmi. "We did have actual revenue coming in from the business-to-business site. At one point we had well over one hundred customers who were paying for our content. Sometimes it would be small, and they'd pay a few hundred dollars, or sometimes a few thousand dollars, but we did have actual money coming in the doors."

AtomFilms also spent a lot of money on marketing in the beginning. "We had TV ads, so we also managed to blow a lot of our money quickly," says Salmi. "It was somewhat of an arms race. We felt that we could either sit back and be conservative or we could try to compete with a lot of heavy hitters in Hollywood. We decided to compete, but that cost us money. We lost some money, but we didn't become an also-ran. Fortunately, we did have this core business that sustained us and kept us going."

AtomFilms works a lot with people from Hollywood. "Our intent was to get broad exposure for these films and these filmmakers," says Salmi. "We started out of my love for short films. I always liked working with new artists. I liked dealing with the up-and-comers. So I always wanted to make sure they got exposure in Hollywood."

Salmi says the quickest way to break a new filmmaker is to create something very short, between three to five minutes, that is very popular on the Internet. "That can launch a career right there," says Salmi. "The buzz happens. You might get a newspaper article written about it. It gets passed around through e-mail. And I think that's a great way to launch a career.

"For the Internet, we look for web hits, for something that is quick and people love, and for the subject matter to be a little more out there," says Salmi. "The things that attract the Internet audience tend to be animations, but sometimes they're films and they're very short.

"The other thing we look for are very high-quality films that have won awards, might feature a well-known actor, or someone that's associated with it is well known," continues Salmi. "That can be anything from a two-minute short to something that's thirty minutes long. It would do well on the Internet with people who have broadband connections because they like to watch some of the more quality ones. It would also work well with us selling to HBO and other partners because they're looking for that high quality."

A good example is *Bikini Bandits,* which was randomly submitted to the site. "It's a Roger Corman spoof by way of a girl with guns," says Salmi. "It's a big favorite that we discovered a few years ago. That was by some advertising executives in Philadelphia, and it was their first short. It was one of those random submissions that came in the mail and I said, 'Hmmm, this is interesting.'"

The submission process to get your film onto AtomFilms is rather simple, and the company receives up to a couple hundred submissions a week. They are accepted by tape or as a digital file, and there is an online form that can be printed out and sent in with the short. "We make sure there are no rights issues with the films," warns Salmi. "We make sure they don't use any kind of music they don't have rights to, for instance, because we're paying filmmakers and we are for profit. We are very careful there."

And they do pay the filmmaker, but they generally ask for a three- to seven-year license in return. "If it's a really hot film, we may pay some kind of upfront advance," says Salmi. "Depending on if we want it just for the Internet or if we want it for broader distribution, we might ask just for Internet rights, North American TV rights, or international rights. Anytime there's any kind of revenue attached to the film, whether it's online and there's advertising with the film, or if it's sold to somebody, we pay a royalty. And that royalty percentage varies quite a bit depending on the film and the distribution channels. It's in the ten to forty percent range of the gross."

Like Hypnotic, AtomFilms has also gotten into the branded entertainment business. "We occasionally produce stuff with a sponsor," says Salmi. "A sponsor wants to produce something that features the sponsor's product. Sometimes we just get a sponsor to pay for the production of a film."

The next evolution of AtomFilms might see the company bringing short form content to television with a twenty-four-hour, seven-day-a-week shorts television channel. Atom Television was launched in 2002, and the company hopes to make it a reality in the near future.

FILM FESTIVALS

Film festivals are a great place to screen your film in front of an audience and get recognized. Many of today's top filmmakers got their start by screening their film at a festival and getting discovered. Today, festivals are good for more than just screening films. Deals are made. Careers are launched. And stars are born.

The Internet sites are not the only companies scouting short films at the film festivals. Hollywood agencies and movie companies are also there looking for hot new filmmaking talent. These days there are so many film festivals, how do you know where to go?

"If you want to get exposed to Los Angeles and New York, enter festivals that are as close to LA and New York as possible," suggests Steve Hein. "Sure, there are the big ones—Sundance, Toronto, Cannes—but not everybody can get into those. But if you enter the Mill Valley Film Festival, the Santa Barbara Film Festival, the Long Beach Film Festival, the Hollywood Short Film Festival . . . people in LA and New York go to those because they're within an hour's drive.

"You don't have to get into Sundance. You don't have to get into Toronto. You don't have to get into Telluride," continues Hein. "Getting into the Los Angeles Independent Short Film Festival can give you the same if not better access, because not as many people are competing for the attention. All you need is for one person to really like it and to play godfather for you and get you in the right seat."

"Once you strategically plan which festivals you want to hit, exposure on the festival circuit is great, especially if you're an emerging filmmaker," says Gary Bryman. "You go out there and meet your peers; you go out there and meet other filmmakers who are doing what you're doing and developing new projects."

When Bryan Gordon made *Ray's Male Heterosexual Dance Hall,* he did not realize the film would go to festivals all around the world. "Back then no one really thought about it because it wasn't something that ever really happened that much" says Gordon. "Today, with all the awards around the clock for everything, people are more conscious of it. When it got selected for Sundance, that was like 'Whoa.' Then it got accepted to practically every festival in the world. I went around the world with it. It became a big hit at Sundance. Today it's a cult hit. It plays in Cuba with Fidel Castro as an example of capitalism. It won a gay and lesbian film festival award as best short film back then because they interpreted that it had an underlying homosexuality to it."

Eric Kripke is a firm believer in the film festival circuit, but unlike Hein and Bryman, he feels that it's only the big ones that count. "Film festivals are great and amazing and fun, but if it's not Sundance, Toronto, Cannes, or the U.S. Comedy Arts Festival, they're just nice excuses to travel and meet other filmmakers and exchange war stories," says Kripke. "I'm always in these film festivals and I think there's gonna be someone in the audience, but that's just not the case. The fun is in the purity of loving movies, but except the festivals I mentioned, they're not career boosters at all."

Gene Klein cites Sundance and Slamdance as the best festivals for short filmmakers. "They look for films that have a distinct point of view," says Klein. "Those are the people who end up being able to make their way in the world. The problem with films with a distinct point of view is that they can sometime be polarizing. They really like them or they really hate them. I tend to think that's a really great thing. Getting that strong a reaction from people either way is probably a great thing, as long as that reaction isn't blahh."

For a listing of film festivals with shorts competitions, please see Appendix III.

ANCILLARY MARKETS

There are many more outlets for the distribution of short films. Commercial and pay TV, airplanes, and even direct sell through on VHS and DVD are just some of the ways short films are distributed. These avenues mean good news for short filmmakers who now, more than ever, have several options for the distribution of their work.

Before Gene Klein came to Hypnotic, he worked at HBO for a number of years in film programming, buying features for HBO and Cinemax. While there, he started traveling to film festivals and through the process of screening features saw a lot of shorts. "I started to see these big, broad, well done, very commercial works that I thought would be perfect for HBO and Cinemax—they didn't seem to be the kind of short that folks like the Sundance Channel would be interested in," says Klein. "So I put a little proposal together for HBO to carve out a small shorts budget and fill some odd time programming needs."

At the time, HBO and Cinemax had "anchored programming," meaning a movie would finish at ten after the hour, but nothing else would begin until the half-hour. Klein thought the stations could fill this time by showing a short followed by ten minutes of promos. Klein put the proposal together, it was approved, and it soon became a reality.

As vice president of distribution, one of Susan Peterson's duties at Hypnotic is to find ancillary markets to license short films to. "I have an understanding after working with different channels, both here in the United States and all over the world, and know what their audiences and sensibilities are," says Peterson. "I look for things specific to them. But there are always going to be your top ten to twenty short films that everybody is going to want."

A good example of that is a short film called *Zen and the Art of Landscaping,* which was a Student Academy Award winner. "You're going to find a lot of longevity with Student Academy Award winners and those types of films," says Peterson. "It comes down to all the things that make great TV shows and features: great story, writing, good acting, and—my personal preference—the production values have to be pretty good. You don't want it to stand out as an amateur piece of work."

There are many different outlets that need short-form programming. "Pay television channels are the first place," says Peterson. "People licensed shorts initially because it was interstitial material [that was shown between full-length programs] so they could round out their programming schedules. We sell across all platforms worldwide. That's airlines, TV, video on demand, wireless, and pretty much everything else. Theatrical is less prevalent. We do know that shorts have a pretty good run in the festival circuit. That's sort of their theatrical side."

PROFITABILITY

Apparently there is an entire business structure for short films. But at the end of the day, are short films a viable source of income to filmmakers? Steve Hein says, "No. Do some people make their money back? Yes. *Battle of the Sexes* made its money back through foreign sales and tape sales. *George Lucas in Love* made its money back. *Peep Show* did, and a handful of others have made their money and a very small profit. But you're doing a short as an investment in yourself, not as an asset."

Producers like Hein and Jana Sue Memel continue to produce shorts, despite the fact that they will never get rich off them. One of the business models these producers use is to produce a short film for a young director so that ostensibly they will then be attached to produce that person's next feature-length project. But it is a risk. Many of these follow-up features never get off the ground.

Still, there are other reasons. "Our very first film won an Oscar," says Memel. "We were nominated every year for the first three or four years. And where more development people I knew spent a lot of time eating lunch, and if they were lucky a movie would get made every two years, I was in production for five years. And I was making movies. And I loved telling stories. I was never not doing that.

"We ran our company at a deficit, which to some account we still do," continues Memel. "Even to this day, the thing I love most is making short movies. There's no studio notes. There's no 'Hire this actor because of these box-office reasons.' It's truly in some sense the purest form of filmmaking and because of how, in essence, with no money certainly by Hollywood terms, you get the opportunity to beg and borrow stuff that, even if you had a little money you couldn't get, so these shorts look like spectacularly large films. So for me as a filmmaker, it's really everything anybody who doesn't aspire to have big cars and big houses could want."

GEORGE LUCAS IN LUCK

And of course, sometimes the planets align and a short film really launches a filmmaker into the stratosphere. "We hit the jackpot," says director Joe Nussbaum. "We were right there with the right product for the right audience at the exact moment. People just were getting faster connections.

Every news outlet was saying the new big thing is watching movies on your computer. Short films were the only thing people had the real bandwidth to stomach. They couldn't download full movies. Every website in the world was popping up—AtomFilms, IFilm, etc.

"To make the planets really align, we had a *Star Wars* parody. And who loves the Internet more than sci-fi geeks? And so our audience on the Internet was huge. So we made a lucrative deal with a startup company called mediatrip.com, and they launched their website and put us right in the centerpiece of it. Millions of people watched our short online. It was phenomenal. It was incredible. It was so successful that we combined with Mediatrip to sell the videotape. We sold it on amazon.com, and we've sold like fifty thousand videos to date. We were the number-one-selling video on Amazon for the better part of three months. We put together a DVD presentation with three other Mediatrip shorts, and we sold another fifteen to twenty thousand copies on DVD. We made our money back more than twofold.

"We've also sold it to airlines and foreign TV," continues Nussbaum. "We sold it to the Sci-Fi Channel, and they put it on their show *Exposure*. That deal was worth almost half the budget. We've done really well with it, but whenever I talk to anyone, especially aspiring short filmmakers, and I get to this part of the story, I tell them in no uncertain terms, do not do this to make your money back. You won't do it. I did not do this to make my money back. I had no dream in the world that I would make my money back. I wanted to make my money back through salaries I'd make as a director, not through actual money that would come in from the short. That was just a miracle."

Ultimately, Joe Nussbaum's story is an example of, literally, a Hollywood ending. By making the right film at the right time and getting it in front of the right people, his short opened a lot of doors in the entertainment business. The next chapter will share some more short film success stories. With a lot of hard work, some savvy filmmaking, and a little luck, it could happen to you, too.

11

Landing the Deal:
Let the Hard Work Pay Off

"When you're doing your own film—a short film or a festival film—you get to do exactly what you want to do. When you're working on a studio film, the hardest part is working with other people. That's the biggest difference between doing a festival film and doing a studio film. There's just a lot more people involved."

—Mike Mitchell, director

SOMETHING IN COMMON

The filmmakers interviewed in this book all have something in common. They were all able to launch successful filmmaking careers off the success of a short film. But for every one who has succeeded, there are hundreds of others who have not been as lucky.

It has not been an easy ride for any of these filmmakers. Just because you are given an opportunity to direct a feature, there is no guarantee your film will ever get made. Some of these talented filmmakers are still waiting for their shot.

Having a successful short is just the beginning. It opens doors. But now the real work begins. How do you use this opportunity to launch your career?

Steve Hein and Gary Bryman produce short films for very specific reasons, and that is typically to launch a property or launch a filmmaker. "It's very much a sales tool," says Hein. "We have a lot of the same requirements that people look for in a feature film: something that might be higher concept, a filmmaker who has an original voice and an interesting perspective. There are a lot of short films that are very good that are produced as student films or made out of passion that we would not make because the shorts we produce are for a very specific purpose, and that is to get a property or an individual known in the studio system."

Gene Klein, vice president of acquisitions for Hypnotic Films, has a different opinion. "What people shouldn't do is make a short film and try to calculate what's going to make the film good for their career. I think they have to create it from a very pure place," says Klein. "The best short films are the ones that go for it, that tell unusual stories, that develop unusual characters, or that take a chance and come straight from the heart.

"Short films can launch careers," says Klein. "But when you're choosing your subject matter, choose subject matter that means something to you as a writer/director. For example, if your personality and personal taste tend toward the thriller and darker material and that's what you've been writing in terms of your feature scripts, you're going to work in that general area for your short as well for a couple reasons. One, it's a comfort zone for the creative person. But two, it also helps you set up the next thing."

Assuming you can get to that level and you can get somebody's attention with your short, the next question is always going to be, "What's next? What else do you have?" "It's easiest for people if there's a line to be drawn between the short you've made and the other material you have," says Klein. "If you did a dark thriller as a short and you have a comedy script, there's a little bit of a disconnect for people."

PROCEED WITH CAUTION

Jana Sue Memel offers these tips for making a short to launch your career. "Don't do something you've seen before. Don't use any voiceover. Don't make film noir. Go to six different university filmmaking programs, look at everything, and don't do anything like that. Over and over and over again, people make the same shorts. They all have different stories and different actors, but there's nothing unique about them. The way you launch your career is by doing something unique as a filmmaker, whether it's a short or a twenty-six-thousand-dollar feature, the thing to do is make sure you're doing something unique. It's truly that simple.

"If you're not in film school of some sort, you have to find a way to get your unique thing seen," says Memel. "Fifty percent of it is make something unique. The other fifty percent of it is how you get people to see your unique work. One is being in the right city. Two is knowing the right people. Three is networking and getting it seen. The getting it seen part is actually more important than what you make. If you make it and only your parents watch it, you don't have a career."

Memel warns against the hype of short filmmakers who make a short and then land a studio deal from that one sample of work. "Most of those people have crashed and burned at picture one," says Memel. "I think by and large, the people who haven't might not have made any shorts that you know about but have been sitting at home with their VHS cameras since they were eight years old. I don't think filmmakers burst on the scene having never thought about being a filmmaker before, take one night class, somebody puts a camera in their hand, and lo and behold they're at the doors of Paramount Studios.

"To be able to direct actors effectively, frame pictures in such a way that it's intriguing and command large groups of people to follow you through the fire requires a force of personality, and character, and artistic integrity that means you're not just a poseur. The people who crash and burn haven't learned how to work in the system because a lot of it has to do with either politics and compromise and not so much with filmmaking. So the short that was brilliant that led to a studio deal is perhaps a portrayal of their real art form. But it doesn't talk to their ability to stand the tides of studio politics."

The rest of this chapter will focus on the real success stories of many of the filmmakers featured in this book. Consider these case studies as lessons to learn by and goals to aspire to. The true success can only be measured in time, through longevity of career. But these filmmakers are certainly off to a great start!

Eduardo Rodriguez
Daughter
Outcome: Three-Picture deal with Dimension Films

Eduardo Rodriguez was getting ready to graduate from Florida State University. His student visa was about to expire, and he thought that if he did not get a job, he was going to have to return to Venezuela. Before that happened, Rodriguez planned to move to Los Angeles to see if he could find a job in the film business.

While making plans to head west to California, one of Rodriguez's film professors asked him to stay in town to help with the sound design for a movie he had shot called *Vampire Rock*. Because Rodriguez needed a job, he agreed to take on the position and remain in Tallahassee for a short while longer. Rodriguez figured once his work on the movie was completed, he would then go to Los Angeles as planned.

At the same time Rodriguez was designing sound for the movie in Florida, the film school held a screening of student films at the Directors Guild of America in Los Angeles. Rodriguez's film *Daughter* was among the shorts screened. Right away, his phone started to ring. Various agents and managers wanted to represent the young filmmaker based on the strength of his short.

While Rodriguez was working on *Vampire Rock*, he had started developing ideas for other screenplays with a friend. "I already had calls from agents, and I wanted to have something to show them," says Rodriguez. "Whatever we were going to write, we needed to write in a month because I was going to LA and I wanted to have it done before I went. We started working on a script, and we finished the whole thing in twenty days."

Once Rodriguez finished the script, he set a date to move to Los Angeles to start meeting with potential handlers. But then Rodriguez received another call that would change his life. The caller was Bob Weinstein, chairman of Dimension Films. He asked Rodriguez what he wanted to do next. "I want to keep making movies," Rodriguez responded. He then told Weinstein of his plan to fly to Los Angeles to meet with these agents.

According to Rodriguez, the rest of his conversation with Weinstein went like this: " 'I'd love to talk to you. Do you mind instead of going to LA if I fly you here to New York? We can talk and then I will fly you anywhere you want to go. If you still want to go to LA, I'll send you to LA.' "

Rodriguez quickly responded, "Yes, of course I want to go to New York."

Weinstein asked the young director if he had any projects he would like to do next. Rodriguez told him about the script he had just completed. " 'I don't know if I want to send it to you because I don't even know if it's a good script.' And he said, 'Send it to me. It doesn't matter because I just want to read it so we have something else to talk about.' "

The script was called *Symbiosis,* and it was based on another of Rodriguez's student films. He sent the script to Weinstein. Later that week, Rodriguez flew to New York to meet the studio head. "I wasn't nervous, but when I got to the airport in New York, I threw up," admits Rodriguez. "They had a car waiting for me that took me to the meeting. They asked me if I wanted anything. 'Yes, where's the bathroom?' So I went and threw up again. Then I met [Dimension president] Andrew Rona. He was the one who calmed me down."

Rona accompanied Rodriguez to the restaurant to meet Bob Weinstein. "We talked about movies," remembers Rodriguez. "What movies do you like? What movies do you not like? What do you want to do? We talked about *Symbiosis,* and one of the things that surprised me was that he actually liked the script. He wanted to make it."

Weinstein told Rodriguez that the script had some problems and needed to be rewritten. He reminded the studio chief that he had written it in twenty days. "He asked me, 'Do you want to make *Symbiosis?*' I told him, 'Yeah, I do want to make *Symbiosis.*' He said, 'I want to make it, too.' That was when we sealed the deal."

Rodriguez later found out that he had been offered a three-picture deal from Dimension Films. "You expect to read that in a magazine about someone else," says Rodriguez. "But you never actually expect that, so all this stuff has been very, very nice, but at the same time very surreal."

Rodriguez considers himself the luckiest guy in the world. He still cannot figure out how he came into this good fortune. "I'm still asking myself, why me?" says Rodriguez. "I don't have an answer for that. There are a lot of factors. You have to work hard to get to do what you want to do. I think luck is another element because a lot of people work hard and not a lot of people get exactly what they want. The fact that Bob Weinstein liked *Daughter* was not just because it was a good movie, but also because he woke up that day and wanted to see *Daughter.* Something just clicked that day at that moment with that guy."

With a deal already on the table, Rodriguez continued on to Los Angeles to meet with agents. Now everyone was after the young filmmaker. But his decision had already been made. Rodriguez signed with ICM. "They were one of the guys I was going to talk with before this thing with Miramax happened," says Rodriguez. "They called me and were very excited about the movie. They believed in me because they saw the movie before the whole Dimension thing happened. That was a nice thing because you don't want somebody who just was there because you already got a job. You want someone who was there because they believe in you."

Rodriguez is currently rewriting *Symbiosis,* which he hopes to have in production in the near future.

Mike Mitchell

Herd

Outcome: Successful studio feature director

Mike Mitchell is a great example of why it is important for young filmmakers to have jobs working in the industry. Having gone to school at Cal Arts, Mitchell's early jobs were in animation. He made valuable contacts while gaining experience in both animation and storytelling in general.

While working at various animation companies, Mitchell enjoyed experimenting on the weekends by making his own short films. "I felt that I was learning more if I did it myself," says Mitchell. "All the mistakes were mine."

Mitchell's work on these animated shorts helped him hone his filmmaking abilities. "Every time I made a festival film I would use it as a calling card, and it would always kick me up a notch to get me a better job," says Mitchell. "I did this cartoon that showed at Sundance before *Boxing Helena* called *Frannie's Christmas,* and that helped more than anything to get good jobs in animation."

Although Mitchell was conscious of the fact that these shorts could actually help him, he really just made them for fun. Another of his early shorts was called *Chunks of Life.* It was made with puppets, and it, too, was shown at Sundance. ABC picked it up, developed a TV show, and actually made a pilot. But unfortunately, it never went any farther.

For Mitchell, the third time was the charm. His third short, *Herd,* played at the Slamdance Film Festival. It got a great deal of attention, especially from the management team of Chris Bender and J. C. Spink. Bender and Spink started to circulate the tape and got a copy to Adam Sandler, who in turn got a copy to producer Sid Gannis. They both thought it was really funny.

Before Mitchell knew what was happening, the pair offered him an opportunity to direct a $15 million studio feature. Mitchell believes he was being given this incredible chance, not so much because of the strength of *Herd* or even his other shorts, but because the studio found out that he had worked in the industry before and had experience working for other directors such as Spike Jonze and Henry Selick.

"I had been in meetings before about movies, but nothing happened," says Mitchell. "So I went into the meeting not thinking anything would happen. In the meeting, I said a few ideas for jokes and gags. That was it."

Soon thereafter, Mitchell got a phone call telling him he had the job. "I was terrified," admits Mitchell. "It was already moving so quickly that I didn't even have a chance to think about it. They had already hired a pro-

were confident. We knew there was a feature film worth of story there, which we set about working out."

Once Lord had the idea, he approached DreamWorks as well as the other studios. "We had a very good calling card," says Lord. "We had three Oscars. We had some great short films. And we had a great idea. We put that package together, and it was easy from that position. But it won't be easy for everybody. I know that."

Having made a name for himself in animation, Lord had, in fact, previously been approached by Hollywood to do a feature film a number of times. "We're an exceptional case," says Lord. "We did something special. We did something that wasn't like mainstream animation but it was widely known, especially *Wallace and Gromit*. So we were approached by Walt Disney, long before DreamWorks, and later we talked with all the studios. So I felt very confident. I knew they wanted us because we had something to offer.

"If you do something very well, even with short films, studios need that," says Lord. "Studios need the great new director, the great new writer, the great new designer. Where are they going to come from, except out of film school, or out of making short films? And we were confident in what we had to offer, and it turned out that we were right. People were prepared to trust us."

Now that *Chicken Run* has become a success, there are plans for additional features. "We chose to have a five-picture deal to make more pictures, partly because we wanted to build up the studio," says Lord. "When we did *Chicken Run,* the studio grew from about one-hundred people to about three-hundred. We're currently invested in the idea of keeping the studio always with a round number of people employed, more like three-hundred, and doing a sequence of films with DreamWorks if that works out. To be honest, I slightly regret the loss of independence that we have bought into. But they've given us enormous financial backing that we couldn't get anywhere else."

Eric Kripke
Battle of the Sexes
Outcome: Successful screenwriting career, TV show creator, still wants to direct a feature

Eric Kripke made *Truly Committed* when he was twenty-two years old. For whatever reason, it was not opening the doors to Hollywood he had hoped it would. "It was a good film, but it has to be great," says Steve Hein, who produced the short for Kripke.

Kripke thinks the main reason *Truly Committed* did not explode was it was too long. "It was a sixteen-minute short film," says Kripke. "[It should be] under ten for sure, and ten is long. I've never heard anyone in the history of man walk out of a short film because it was too short. No one ever says that. They're always too long. If you're making a short film to express yourself artistically, go nuts. You can make it as long as you want. But if you're looking to create a calling card within the film industry, five minutes is great.

"I hate to be this crassly commercial, but most people aren't going to see it in a screening room," continues Kripke. "Most people are going to have a videotape they pop into the VCR in their office in the couple minutes they have before a meeting, so you have to grab them fast. And you have to let them go in five minutes with a good taste in their mouth and send them off to their next meeting. I think [four-and-a-half-minute] *Battle of the Sexes* for me was much more of a career booster than *Truly Committed*. *Truly Committed* got a good reaction. People enjoyed it. It went to film festivals. It had a great run. But *Battle of the Sexes* changed my career."

Battle of the Sexes was a comedic look at what really goes on behind closed doors when women enter the restroom. To coincide with their grassroots campaign to send out the short, Kripke had written a screenplay he wanted to direct as well. "We thought he should follow that up with something because once the town sees your film, you only have one real window of opportunity before the next step comes along," explains

Hein. "So in that six-month window when you finish something, you've really got to strike when the iron is hot. The smartest thing is to be generating your own material. People want to make the movie based on the quality of the project or the material, so you have a piece in your hand that justifies why you're attached to direct it."

This time they got closer. A great deal of interest. A lot of positive feedback. And then nothing. "Back to the drawing board. Another two years," says Kripke. "It was over and done, we had hung up our hat. Well, we gave it our all. There's nothing to be ashamed of. But then we got one of those eleventh-hour calls. DreamWorks said they were not going to buy this script, but they really loved the writing and they dug the short, and asked it I would like a two-picture screenwriting deal. I was like, 'I would like that very much.' After that, my agent set up a ton of meetings. Two or three weeks of two to three meetings a day. You just meet everybody. It's fun and it's a whirlwind. You're the new virgin at prom.

"I got a screenwriting deal! I'm a working Hollywood professional," says Kripke. "And my family's calling me. I'm getting gift baskets from people. It's like some weird Hollywood bar mitzvah kind of thing. And [DreamWorks executive] Adam Goodman said to me something to the effect of, 'As hard as it was to get to where you are now, now it really gets hard.' And he's so right. It's such a challenging business."

Kripke looked at the DreamWorks deal as a huge step up in getting to the next level of his career. "It's funny how quickly it happened," says Kripke. "Between the time I first got into Sundance to where I had a deal with DreamWorks, it was probably a total of five or six weeks. What's amazing is that I was busting my ass for two years generating material, and that's the advice I would give, too. Just keep working and keep creating material because the only thing you can control as a filmmaker is the quality of your material and being a vibrant, creative force. The thing you can't control is when that weird bizarre window of fate and luck suddenly converge at the right time at the right moment. And you have no control over that. So all you can do is keep working, and that's what I did."

At DreamWorks, Kripke wrote a sci-fi comedy called *Little Green*

Men. But he had not given up on his desire to direct. After landing the deal, Kripke signed with Endeavor. The agency sent out his short film for open directing assignments, and if the producers and studio executives responded, they would set up a meeting for Kripke to pitch his take on their material. "I would bust my ass on these pitches because I figured it was the only way [to get the job] by working harder than the next guy," says Kripke. "I would work days and days and have seven single-spaced typed pages and photo samples, and I'd have a sketch artist sketch out designs. I got to be the pitch everyone loved to hear, but I never got the job. The reality in Hollywood is, you're really lucky if you average one 'Yes' for every fifteen to twenty 'No's.' So you just work through the 'No's' to get to the 'Yes.'"

After many pitches, Kripke landed a job. He got attached to direct a movie at MGM called *Munchies.* "*Munchies* was a long process, and MGM got to the point where they gave me a shot," says Kripke. "We were doing script revisions. We hired a casting director. We had a line producer. We were putting together our schedule. And then, someone at MGM didn't like the script and when it came time to spend a lot of money . . . it sort of evaporated."

Luckily, Kripke was building a solid reputation for himself as a screen-writer. When most filmmakers would have to go back to waiting tables, Kripke was getting hired for various rewriting jobs. It also gave him some time to focus on his own writing. "I wrote an independent film, which is where my passion really is," says Kripke. "I want to get back to my short film roots, to get a million dollars together and just shoot the thing."

Kripke's independent film might have to wait. He has had a very busy year. This past year, he sold two pitches: one to Columbia Pictures with Neil Moritz producing, the other to 20th Century Fox that is being produced by Steve Hein, Gary Bryman, and Barry Josephson. In addition, Kripke created the new version of *Tarzan* for the WB. Yet all this success is bittersweet.

"Here's where I am with my career," says Kripke. "Screenwriting is doing very well. I'm working a lot. I also wrote a horror script [*Boogey-*

man] that Steve [Hein] and Gary [Bryman] are the executive producers of and the producers are Sam Raimi and Rob Tappert. They're shooting in February, so my first movie's gonna get shot. And my TV show got shot. Next year all the stuff that's going into production will be made, and it will all be out there. So the good news is I'm so lucky to be working and to have stuff going into production. I appreciate that for what it is.

"On the other hand, I'm not on set," says Kripke. "I'm not shooting. And when I was eight years old I didn't say I wanted to be locked away behind my computer pale and pasty. I wanted to be on a set directing movies. Frankly, I need to shoot some more. I'm itchy to shoot. By the time the book comes out, I'll be back on the set sinking my money into something.

"At the time I was really sweating, 'What's going to be the right career move?'" says Kripke. "But there's a completely other way to look at it, which is it's just cool to be on set and it's cool to be working with good people and it's cool to be setting up shots. And I sort of miss that. And I miss that camaraderie. And I'm at the point now where I want to shoot because I live for that. And that's the stuff I'm passionate about."

Trevor Sands

Inside

Outcome: Two-picture deal with Dimension Films

When Trevor Sands announced to his agents that he was going to spend $50,000 of his own money to make a short film, they were a little apprehensive. "They understood that I wanted to be a director," says Sands. "They did not necessarily see what I wanted to do with this particular script. And they did not necessarily see how it was going to get me work."

But ultimately, they were supportive. By the time Sands's agent saw the rough cut of *Inside,* he was genuinely enthusiastic and thought he could work with it. "I think it came from the fear that I was going to come up with something that wasn't that good and then they were going to be in a position of having to shop it around or politely tell me that they could no longer represent me," says Sands. "It's always dangerous as an agent go-ing into a situation where your client's trying to do this big thing and he's spending all this money. You don't want to be rude and tell him it's not go-ing to work. But when it was done, he was happy I had done it because it turned out well."

Although Sands had a sense that it was going to be worthwhile and he could do something impressive, he could not be sure how it would turn out. "You can't account for what might go wrong, and you can't know that it is gonna be what you think it's gonna be," says Sands. "But luckily, I had grown up enough to have a handle on what is fantasy versus reality. I wasn't twenty years old trying to do this. I was twenty-seven years old. Once you get to be that age, you better shut up and do it—and do it as well as it can be done or you're not good enough to do it and you might as well do something else.

"When you're twenty, you're just impressed that you're making a movie, and if it's not that good it's because you're twenty," says Sands, re-ferring to the feature he directed at that young age. "In that sense, forty thousand dollars spent at age twenty-seven is better money spent than two hundred thousand dollars spent at age twenty because I had the experi-ence and maturity to know what I was getting into and handled it as best as it could be handled. So I increased my chances of success and ended up with a product that I'm proud of."

Finishing his short has presented many new opportunities to Sands. "My agent sends me scripts that are open directing assignments," says Sands. "The William Morris Agency really got behind it. They toured the film to all the studios. They screened it for the executives. It definitely put me in the place that if I had a script that a studio wanted to make, this film would make them more inclined to attach me as director.

"It did establish me to some degree as a voice in the community," con-tinues Sands. "If you go out with a spec and you're attached to direct, people will usually roll their eyes. It's something that's seen as this annoy-ing side note, and people are figuring they'll get you off the project later.

But if you have a short film that's respectable, people won't roll their eyes as much and they'll take a more serious look at it."

But ultimately, the big payoff from the film came from Bob Weinstein, who gave Sands a writing and directing deal at Dimension Films. "He was given the film by one of his executives," says Sands. "Bob watched it and said, 'I like this guy. Keep him on the radar.' A month later, I came in and pitched my take on *The Six Million Dollar Man* to [executive] Michael Zoumis. Zoumis liked my take and brought me in to [co-heads of production] Brad [Weston] and Andrew [Rona], who liked my take and then set up an immediate meeting with Bob Weinstein.

"Bob heard my take on *The Six Million Dollar Man*, decided that was the one he wanted to go with, and gave me that job to write the movie," says Sands. "But because he had already seen *Inside* and knew I wanted to direct and thought I could direct, he asked his legal department to negotiate into the deal an additional project that I would be attached to direct after *The Six Million Dollar Man*." Sands got what he wanted.

Joe Nussbaum
George Lucas in Love
Outcome: Attached to direct seven studio features; none have yet gone into production

Joe Nussbaum still remembers showing the rough cut of *George Lucas in Love* to friends for the very first time. "I showed the rough cut to someone, and they didn't really laugh at all," recalls Nussbaum. "Then right when it was over, they go, 'Let me see it again.' Then we started showing it to people and they were like 'This is great.' We quickly learned that in general people were liking it a lot. People were giving it to other people, and crazy things were happening."

Everything came together rather quickly. Nussbaum signed with a manager and an agent. "Having interest from the agencies was amazing," says Nussbaum. "Hearing about agencies where the whole agency watched it in their company meeting. Hearing from friends in development who would call me to tell me, 'Your tape just showed up on my desk.' It was the most exciting time ever for me. I would literally call to check my messages and hear, 'Joe. It's Mike Ovitz calling.' And it really was Mike Ovitz—it wasn't a friend playing a prank."

Nussbaum wanted to capitalize on the film's success right away, but he needed a plan. "I just tried to weigh the opportunities as best I could and sign with good people," says Nussbaum. "I signed with a good agent and manager. I'm still with them. I still feel great about them. I was able to sign with a commercial production company, and I've directed thirty commercials to date. I've done commercials for ESPN, Kellogg's, Nike, Tropicana, Gain laundry detergent, etc., and I've been lucky enough and unlucky enough to tell you that I've been attached to seven feature films."

Like his fellow filmmakers, being attached to direct a project and actually going into production are two completely separate things. "I'll tell you the sob stories of why none of them have gone to the big screen," sighs Nussbaum. "DreamWorks was one of the most receptive places right away. Spielberg himself really took a liking to the film. He sent it to Lucas. They hired me to do a movie called *Almost Romantic,* which then went into turnaround.

"Then I was signed on to direct a movie called *Special* at MGM which fell apart," says Nussbaum. "Then I met at Imagine with Ron Howard and was hired to direct *How To Eat Fried Worms* for Nickelodeon and Paramount, and that went into turnaround. Then I was hired by Landscape, an independent company, to do a movie called *Romantic Comedy,* which then switched to MGM and I was off the project. Then I set something up with Tim Dowling and Joseph Levy called *Come Back to Me* at Senator. The option has just expired. Then, last spring, I was hired to direct another movie at MGM, called *I Want Kandee.* We were casting that this summer. We even made an offer to an actress, and now that's in limbo."

But there are still some projects Nussbaum is attached to that are on the horizon. "One is a project that is called *The Perfect Man* over at Warner Bros. The writers are still working on a new draft," says Nussbaum. "On one hand I've been so lucky. I've walked into the room and been hired to do movies seven times, which is unbelievable. My own management and agents can't believe it. People say that open directing assignments are the hardest thing to get. They say it's much easier to generate your own material. I've gotten these jobs, but I can't get them into production. Hopefully that can't last."

Luke Greenfield
The Right Hook
Outcome: Successful studio feature director

Luke Greenfield was one of the lucky ones. His student film caught the attention of Hollywood agents, and he signed with ICM right out of film school. But that is where his luck ran out. After several rounds of meetings with Hollywood production companies, nothing materialized, and Greenfield fell into a deep depression.

Greenfield had been making movies since he was ten years old. But there was a dark period after college where he literally stopped making films because he just did not have any money. He and his girlfriend worked together as runners for the post-production department at Viacom delivering dailies tapes to producers. At night, they would write screenplays. "There was no room for living or having fun," says Greenfield. "I was so driven to make a film that I couldn't begin being normal until I was settled in my career."

When that job ended, they worked as temps at Disney Interactive doing data entry, punching in numbers for eight hours a day. "It was killing my soul," says Greenfield. "These were the worst years I ever had. And no matter how bad it gets now—and believe me, there's tough times in making movies—I would look back at these years and be grateful."

Part of Greenfield's frustration was that he felt like he was a failure. "I was watching all these young guys make it from commercials and music videos. And that was a world that no one would let me in. I tried so hard to make a music video. I didn't have the money to make a spec."

After a series of false starts and frustrations, he began collaborating with some friends on *Echo Lake,* which led to the making of his short, *The Right Hook.* For the complete story, see Chapter Three: *Budget.*

With the short film in the can, Luke was working feverishly to edit *The Right Hook.* He was very pleased with the way it was turning out. Greenfield's producer, Juan Castro, knew some people at a management company called MBST. Jonathan Brandstein at MBST wanted to represent Greenfield on the strength of the rough cut of *The Right Hook.* "There was no doubt in his mind, after seeing the rough cut on video, that he could get me a studio feature film," says Greenfield. Brandstein kept begging him every day to show the short to studio executives he knew. But Greenfield was not ready. He did not yet have his follow-up script completed.

Brandstein was tenacious. "He scared me," admits Greenfield. "He kept saying, 'Luke, there's an actors' strike coming up. If you take another year to write your feature screenplay, you might lose your window.' That was my plan, to take the time and hold *The Right Hook* back, write the feature screenplay, and have it ready to go. So it terrified me."

Brandstein finally convinced Greenfield to let him show the unfinished short to at least one person. Greenfield agreed, and Brandstein showed it to Greg Silverman, an executive at Revolution Studios. Within hours, Silverman showed it to Todd Garner, president of production. "Todd Garner loved the short, called me at home, sent me the script for *The Animal,* and said 'I need to meet you tomorrow.' I read the script, and as I turned the pages, a lot of things made me laugh. It was definitely a broad comedy, and it was definitely a tone I knew I could direct."

The next day, Greenfield met Garner, Rob Schneider, and producer Jack Giarraputo. "I had only read the script once, and I usually memorize my pitches for meetings," admits Greenfield, who explained his visual style and how he would make the movie. But I looked Rob in the eye and said 'I will work my ass off on this movie. No one will work harder than me. I'll work 24-7.' And Rob really responds to that."

After just one more meeting with Schneider and the executives, Greenfield got the movie. "I remember Rob saying, 'You've got the job, kid.' And then, twenty minutes later, I was brought into the art department looking at locations and going on location scouts. I had read the script once. They were way in preproduction. They were seven weeks out. Everyone was there except for the DP. It was insanity. I had to do everything against what I believed in, as far as being organized and prepared as possible. There was no time. Plus, this was the first time in my life I was directing something I didn't write. That was very challenging for me, to take someone else's vision. At [Adam Sandler's production company] Happy Madison, they have their own way of making movies and it really works for them. It's a collaboration, and I mean a collaboration. Those guys work it all out together.

"I was the luckiest person alive," continues Greenfield. "There was a day in August I remember driving back. I had made a twenty-eight-thousand-dollar short, and I was about to direct a twenty-five million dollar feature. Unheard of! I was the happiest man alive. I was also the most terrified man alive. So much work needed to be done. To be thrown into a movie that big with these huge visual effects, luckily I had very strong people behind me."

For Greenfield, *The Animal* was really an education in politics. "It wasn't about learning filmmaking, it was about learning about studio politics and about how studio films work," says Greenfield. "It was a great, great, great learning experience. The positives were you had everything at your disposal as far as equipment and money and crew. You could do what you want. The negatives for me were you had no freedom. If you wanted to do something, you had to talk about it with everyone. Exactly why you were putting a camera there, exactly why you were shooting it this way, it was all about talking it over with the group, figuring things out, which is the way many studio films work, especially with a first-time director."

The Animal grossed $58 million domestically. By all accounts, it was a huge success. After *The Animal,* Greenfield set up several other projects, but he still feels that it is his short, not his successful feature, that is responsible for these opportunities. "*The Right Hook* has done everything for me," says Greenfield.

Greenfield attributes careful choices to longevity in the business. After *The Animal,* he wanted to be sure his next project would be different in tone. "I was offered every broad comedy in the world, and my agents and managers kept telling everyone that he's not that guy, so forget it," says Greenfield. "They'd say, 'Who's he want to be?' I don't want to be anyone, but I want to make movies that are unforgettable."

Greenfield's follow-up to *The Animal* is a smaller film called *The Girl Next Door.* "A lot of people think I'm taking a step back and I'm not working with big movie stars, but it's going to prove to the world that I'm not a broad comedy guy and I can do something more in the character-driven drama/comedy vein," says Greenfield. "I could not have been luckier to do *The Animal* and how it came out. And if all of this hadn't worked out the way it did, I don't know what I'd be doing."

Conclusion:
Famous Last Words

"There aren't short filmmakers. There are people who want to be long filmmakers who are making a short to launch their career. Nobody I know, but me, set out to be a short filmmaker—it's not a career."

—Jana Sue Memel, producer

ONE LAST PIECE OF ADVICE

Now that you have read this book, it is time to take what you have learned and implement a plan. Those who came before you stumbled into uncovering the secrets of success. You will benefit by their discoveries.

But also remember that in addition to plotting and planning, at the end of the day, it comes down to that unique creative energy that only you can inject into your project. This is the key factor to carving your niche and making a name for yourself as a filmmaker.

Stay focused on the goal: to become a great filmmaker. This might not be an easy journey, but if you truly believe this is your calling, and you give it 100 percent, I honestly believe you can make it happen. Do not give up. Make an incredible short and launch your filmmaking career.

THE MEETING

It's never quite how you thought it would be. Luke Greenfield had wanted to meet Steven Spielberg for so many years. Ever since his correspondence with the famous director, Greenfield dreamed about the day they would meet. It came sooner than he thought.

Luke Greenfield and about thirty other students were standing in lobby of the Shrine Auditorium donning caps and gowns, ready to receive their diplomas and graduate from USC film school. Out of the blue, two body guards walk up to the group with ear pieces in their ears and ask 'Who's Luke Greenfield?' "I thought I was in trouble," says Greenfield. "I said, 'Look, I didn't do it. I just want to graduate.'"

They escorted Greenfield to this dark hallway around the back of the venue. When they opened the door, there stood Steven Spielberg. "They said, 'Steven, this is Luke. You wrote him a letter when he was sixteen.' And they clapped their hands and left," recalls Greenfield.

"I just have this memory," says Greenfield. "I speak fast and I stutter and mumble normally, but with him I was just so incoherent. And I reminded him who I was. And then I shook his hand when he gave me my diploma. And I looked him in the eye and said thank you for everything. And I never saw him again ever."

FILM SCHOOLS

In the last decade, film schools have sprung up all over the world. There are now many programs to choose from, so be sure to select the one that is best for you. Some of the following schools offer programs specific to various interests such as screenwriting or cinematography, and other programs are more general in nature. Be sure to conduct your due diligence in choosing the program that is right for you.

American Film Institute
2021 North Western Avenue
Los Angeles, CA 90027
323-856-7600
323-367-4578 (fax)
www.afi.com

Boston University
2021 North Western Avenue
Los Angeles, CA 90027
323-856-7600
323-367-4578 (fax)
www.bu.edu/com/filmtv/index.html

Brooklyn College
2900 Bedford Avenue
0314 Plaza Building
Brooklyn, NY 11210
718-951-5664
718-951-4733 (fax)

California State University, Long Beach
University Telecommunications Center (UTC), Room 104
1250 Bellflower Boulevard
Long Beach, CA 90840
562-985-5404
www.csulb.edu

California State University, Northridge
18111 Nordhoff Street
Northridge, CA 91330
818-677-3192
www.cinemaandtelevision.com

Chapman University
School of Film and Television
1 University Drive
Orange, CA 92866
714-997-6765
www.ftv.chapman.edu

College of Santa Fe (Girls Film School)
1600 St. Michaels Drive
Santa Fe, NM 87505
505-473-6409
www.csf.edu/mov

Columbia Academy
1295 West Broadway
Vancouver, B.C. V6H 3X8
Canada
604-736-3316
604-731-5458 (fax)
www.columbia-academy.com

Columbia University
School of the Arts
305 Dodge Hall, Mail Code 1808
2960 Broadway
New York, NY 10027
212-854-2875
www.columbia.edu

Emerson College
120 Boylston Street
Boston, MA 02116
617-824-8801
www.emerson.edu

Flinders University
Anne Rizzo
School of Humanities
GPO Box 2100
Adelaide SA, 5001
Australia
61-8-8201-3908
61-8-8201-3407 (fax)
www.flinders.edu/au

Florida State University
Film School
University Center 3100A
Tallahassee, FL 32306-2350
850-644-7728
850-644-2626 (fax)
filmschool.fsu.edu

Franklin and Marshall College
PO Box 3003
Lancaster, PA 17604-3003
717-291-3911
www.fandm.edu

Full Sail University
3300 University Boulevard
Winter Park, FL 32792
800-226-7625
407-679-6333 (fax)
www.fullsail.com

Griffith University
Gold Coast Campus
PMB50
Gold Coast Mail Centre
Queensland 9726
Australia
61-7-555-28800
www.gu.edu.au/school/fmc

Johns Hopkins University
3400 N. Charles Street, Gilman 146
Baltimore, MD 21218
410-516-5048
410-516-4757 (fax)
www.jhu.edu

Leeds Metropolitan University
The Course Administrator, TV and Film Production
2 Queen Square
Leeds, LS2 8AF
England
44-0-113-283-1900
44-0-113-283-1901 (fax)
www.lmu.ac.uk

Los Angeles Community College (LACC)
855 North Vermont Avenue
Los Angeles, CA 90029
323-953-4000
www.lacc.cc.ca.us

Los Angeles Film School
6363 Sunset Boulevard, Suite 400
Los Angeles, CA 90028
323-860-0789
www.lafilm.com

Middlebury College
Film/Video Studies
Wright Theatre
Middlebury, VT 05753
802-443-3190
www.middlebury.edu

Mount Holyoke College
Film Studies Program
Art Building, Mount Holyoke College
South Hadley, MA 01075
413-538-2200
www.mtholyoke.edu

New York University (NYU)
Film and Television, Undergraduate Division
721 Broadway, 10th Floor
New York, NY 10003
212-998-1700
www.nyu.edu

North Carolina School of the Arts
1533 South Main Street
Winston-Salem, NC 27127-2188
336-770-1338
www.ncarts.edu

Ohio University School of Film
Lindley Hall 378
Athens, OH 45701
740-593-1323
740-593-1328 (fax)
www.cats.ohiou.edu/film/

Pennsylvania State University
Department of Film/Video and Media Studies
129 Carnegie
University Park, PA 16802
814-863-2113
www.psu.edu

Ryerson University
350 Victoria Street
Toronto, Ontario, M5B 2K3
Canada
416-979-5000
www.ryerson.ca

San Diego State University
5500 Campanile Drive
San Diego, CA 92182-4561
619-594-5450
619-594-6246 (fax)
www.sdsu.edu

San Francisco State University
1600 Holloway Avenue
San Francisco, CA 94132
415-338-1629
415-338-0906 (fax)
www.sfsu.edu

Scottsdale Community College
9000 E. Chaparral Road
Scottsdale, AZ 85256
480-423-6000
www.sc.maricopa.edu

Temple University
344 Annenberg Hall
School of Communications and Theater
Philadelphia, PA 19122
215-204-8791
www.temple.edu/fma

University College, Dublin
Room 107, Arts Annexe
University College Dublin
Belfield, Dublin 4
Ireland
353-1-716-8604
353-1-716-8605 (fax)
www.hermes.ucd.ie/~film/

University of Alabama
Box 870152
Tuscaloosa, AL 35487-0152
205-348-6350
205-348-5162 (fax)
www.tcf.ua.edu/grad

University of Barcelona, Spain
FILM-HISTORIA, Center for Cinematic Research
PO Box 12109
Barcelona, 08080
Spain
34-93-333-3466
34-93-449-8510 (fax)
www.swcp.com/~cmora/cine.html

University of California, Berkeley
Program in Film Studies, Dwinelle Hall, #2670
Berkeley, CA 94720
510-642-1415
www.berkeley.edu

University of California, Los Angeles
UCLA Film School
102 E. Melnitz Hall
Box 951622
Los Angeles, CA 90095-1622
310-825-5761
310-825-3383 (fax)
www.tft.ucla.edu

University of California, Santa Barbara
Ellison Hall 1720
Santa Barbara, CA 93106
805-893-2347
805-893-8630 (fax)
www.filmstudies.ucsb.edu

University of California, Santa Cruz
Porter Faculty Services Film and Digital Media Department
1156 High Street
Santa Cruz, CA 95064
831-459-3204
831-459-4008 (fax)
www.arts.ucsc.edu/film/film_frameset.html

University of Central Florida
UCF Department of Film
Communications Building, Room 121
PO Box 163120
Orlando, FL 32816
407-823-FILM (407-823-3456)
www.cas.ucf.edu/film

University of Iowa
425 English-Philosophy Building
Iowa City, IA 52242
319-335-0330
www.uiowa.edu

University of Kansas
The Department of Theatre and Film
356 Murphy Hall
Lawrence, KS 66045
913-864-3511
www.kuhttp.cc.ukans.edu/!theatre/thf.html

University of New Orleans
Department of Drama and Film
Communications Performing Arts Center
New Orleans, LA 70148
504-280-6317
504-280-6318 (fax)
www.uno.edu/~drcom/contactus.html

University of North Texas
RTFP Building, Room 262
PO Box 310589
Denton, TX 76203-0589
940-565-2537
940-369-7838 (fax)
www.rtvf.unt.edu

University of Oklahoma
640 Parrington Oval
Norman, OK 73019
405-325-3020
405-325-7135 (fax)
www.ou.edu/fvs

University of Regina
Department of Media Productions and Studies
3737 Wascana Parkway
Regina, Saskatchewan, S4S 0A2
Canada
www.uregina.ca

University of Southern California
School of Cinema-Television
CTV-G130
Los Angeles, CA 90089-2211
213-740-8358
www-cntv.usc.edu

University of Southern Maine
Media Studies
19 Chamberlain Avenue
Portland, ME 04103
207-780-5972
207-228-8269 (fax)
www.usm.maine.edu

University of Technology, Sydney
PO Box 123
Broadway NSW 2007
Australia
61-2-9514-2285
61-2-9514-1595 (fax)
www.hss.uts.edu.au/departments

University of Texas, Austin
Department of Radio-TV-Film, CMA 6.118
Austin, TX 78712-1091
512-471-4071
512-471-4077 (fax)
www.utexas.edu

University of Toronto
Room 123, Innis College
2 Sussex Avenue
Toronto, Ontario, M5S 1J5
Canada
416-978-7271
www.utoronto.ca/cinema

University of Utah
Division of Film Studies
375 S 1530 E, Room 257b
Salt Lake City, UT 84112-0380
801-581-5127
www.film.utah.edu

University of Victoria
PO Box 1700
Victoria, B.C. V8W 2Y2
Canada
250-721-6306
kafka.uvic.ca/film

University of Wisconsin, Milwaukee
Peck School of the Arts
3203 N. Downer Avenue, MIT B69
Milwaukee, WI 53211
414-229-6015
414-229-5901 (fax)
www.uwm.edu

OSCAR-WINNING SHORTS

Best Animated Short

2002
ChubbChubbs, The directed by: Eric Armstrong

2001
For the Birds directed by: Ralph Eggleston

2000
Father and Daughter produced by: Michael de Wit

1999
Old Man and the Sea, The produced by: Alexander Petrov

1998
Bunny produced by: Chris Wedge

1997
Geri's Game produced by: Jan Pinkava

1996
Quest produced by: Tyron Montgomery, Thomas Stellmach

1995
Close Shave, A produced by: Nick Park

1994
Bob's Birthday produced by: David Fine, Alison Snowden

1993
Wrong Trousers, The produced by: Nick Park

1992
Mona Lisa Descending a Staircase produced by: Joan Gratz

1991
Manipulation produced by: Daniel Greaves

1990
Creature Comforts produced by: Nick Park

1989
Balance produced by: Wolfgang Lauenstein, Christoph Lauenstein

1988
Tin Toy produced by: John Lasseter, William Reeves

1987
Man Who Planted Trees, The produced by: Frederic Back

1986
Greek Tragedy, A produced by: Willem Thijssen, Linda Van Tulden

1985
Anna and Bella produced by: Cilia Van Dijk

1984
Charade produced by: Jon Minnis

1983
Sundae in New York produced by: James Picker

1982
Tango produced by: Zbigniew Rybczynski

1981
Crac produced by: Frederic Back

1980
Fly, The produced by: Ferenc Rofusz

1979
Every Child produced by: Derek Lamb

1978
Special Delivery produced by: Eunice Macaulay, John Weldon

1977
Sand Castle produced by: Co Hoedeman

1976
Leisure produced by: Suzanne Baker

1975
Great produced by: Bob Godfrey

1974
Closed Mondays produced by: Bob Gardiner, Will Vinton

1973
Frank Film produced by: Frank Mouris

1972
Christmas Carol, A produced by: Richard Williams

1971
Crunch Bird, The produced by: Ted Petok

1970
Is It Always Right to Be Right? produced by: Nick Bosustow

1969
It's Tough to Be a Bird produced by: Ward Kimball

1968
Winnie the Pooh and the Blustery Day produced by: Walt Disney

1967
Box, The produced by: Fred Wolf

1966
Herb Alpert and the Tijuana Brass Double Feature produced by: John Hubley,
Faith Hubley

1965
Dot and the Line, The produced by: Les Goldman, Chuck Jones

1964
Pink Phink, The produced by: David DePatie, Friz Freleng

1963
Critic, The produced by: Ernest Pintoff

1962
Hole, The produced by: John Hubley, Faith Hubley

1961
Ersatz (The Substitute) produced by: Herts, Lion International

1960
Munro produced by: William Snyder

1959
Moonbird produced by: John Hubley

1958
Knighty Knight Bugs produced by: John Burton

1957
Birds Anonymous produced by: Edward Selzer

1956
Mister Magoo's Puddle Jumper produced by: Stephen Bosustow

1955
Speedy Gonzales produced by: Edward Selzer

1954
When Magoo Flew produced by: Stephen Bosustow

1953
Toot, Whistle, Plunk and Boom produced by: Walt Disney

1952
Johann Mouse produced by: Frederick Quimby

1951
Two Mouseketeers produced by: Frederick Quimby

1950
Gerald McBoing-Boing produced by: Stephen Bosustow

1949
For Scent-imental Reasons produced by: Edward Selzer

1948
Little Orphan, The produced by: Frederick Quimby

1947
Tweetie Pie produced by: Edward Selzer

1946
Cat Concerto, The produced by: Frederick Quimby

1945
Quiet Please produced by: Frederick Quimby

1944
Mouse Trouble produced by: Frederick Quimby

1943
Yankee Doodle Mouse produced by: Frederick Quimby

1942
Der Fuehrer's Face produced by: Walt Disney

1941
Lend a Paw produced by: Walt Disney

1940
Milky Way produced by: MGM

1939
Ugly Duckling, The produced by: Walt Disney

1938
Ferdinand the Bull produced by: Walt Disney

1937
Old Mill, The produced by: Walt Disney

1936
Country Cousin, The produced by: Walt Disney

1935
Three Orphan Kittens produced by: Walt Disney

1934
Tortoise and the Hare, The produced by: Walt Disney, United Artists

1932/33
Three Little Pigs, The produced by: Walt Disney

1931/32
Flowers and Trees produced by: Walt Disney

Best Live-Action Short

2002
Der er en yndig mand directed by: Marten Strange-Hansen

2001
Accountant, The directed by: Lisa Blount, Ray McKinnon

2000
Quiero Ser (I Want to Be . . .) produced by: Florian Gallenberger

1999
My Mother Dreams the Satan's Disciples in New York produced by: Barbara
Schock, Tammy Tiehel

1998
Election Night (Valgaften) produced by: Anders Jensen, Kim Magnusson

1997
Visas and Virtue produced by: Chris Donahue

1996
Dear Diary produced by: David Frankel, Barry Jossen

1995
Lieberman in Love produced by: Christine Lahti, Jana Sue Memel

1994
Franz Kafka's It's a Wonderful Life produced by: Peter Capaldi, Ruth Kenley-
Letts

1993
Black Rider produced by: Pepe Danquart

1992
Omnibus produced by: Sam Karmann

1991
Session Man produced by: Rob Fried, Seth Winston

1990
Lunch Date, The produced by: Adam Davidson

1989
Work Experience produced by: James Hendrie

1988
Appointments of Dennis Jennings, The produced by: Dean Parisot, Steven Wright

1987
Ray's Male Heterosexual Dance Hall produced by: Jana Sue Memel, Jonathan Sanger

1986
Precious Images produced by: Chuck Workman

1985
Molly's Pilgrim produced by: Jeff Brown

1984
Up produced by: Mike Hoover

1983
Boys and Girls produced by: Janice Platt

1982
Shocking Accident, A produced by: Christine Oestreicher

1981
Violet produced by: Paul Kemp, Shelley Levinson

1980
Dollar Bottom, The produced by: Lloyd Phillips

1979
Board and Care produced by: Ron Ellis, Sarah Pillsbury

1978
Teenage Father produced by: Taylor Hackford

1977
I'll Find a Way produced by: Beverly Shafer, Yuki Yoshida

1976
In the Region of Ice produced by: Andre Guttfreund, Peter Werner

1975
Angel and Big Joe produced by: Bert Salzman

1974
One-Eyed Men Are Kings produced by: Paul Claudon, Edmond Sechan

1973
Bolero, The produced by: William Fertik, Allan Miller

1972
Norman Rockwell's World . . . An American Dream produced by: Richard Barclay

1971
Sentinels of Silence produced by: Robert Amram, Manuel Arango

1970
Resurrection of Broncho Billy, The produced by: John Longenecker

1969
Magic Machines produced by: Joan Stern

1968
Robert Kennedy Remembered produced by: Charles Guggenheim

1967
Place to Stand, A produced by: Christopher Chapman

1966
Wild Wings produced by: Edgar Anstey

1965
Chicken, The produced by: Claude Berri

1964
Casals Conducts: 1964 produced by: Edward Schreiber

1963
Occurrence at Owl Creek Bridge, An produced by: Paul de Roubaix, Marcel Ichac

1962
Heureux Anniversaire produced by: Jean-Claude Carrière, Pierre Etaix

1961
Seawards the Great Ships produced by: Templar Film Studios

1960
Day of the Painter produced by: Ezra Baker

1959
Golden Fish, The produced by: Jacques-Yves Cousteau

1958
Grand Canyon produced by: Walt Disney

1957
Wetback Hound, The produced by: Larry Lansburgh

Best Documentary Short

2002
Twin Towers directed by: Bill Guttentag, Robert David Port

2001
Thoth directed by: Lynn Appelle, Sarah Kernochan

2000
Big Mama produced by: Tracy Seretean

1999
King Gimp produced by: Susan Hadary, William Whiteford

1998
Personals: Improvisations on Romance in the Golden Years, The produced by: Keiko Ibi

1997
Story of Healing, A produced by: Donna Dewey, Carol Pasternak

1996
Breathing Lessons: The Life and Work of Mark O'Brien produced by: Jessica Yu

1995
One Survivor Remembers produced by: Kary Antholis

1994
Time for Justice, A produced by: Charles Guggenheim

1993
Defending Our Lives produced by: Margaret Lazarus, Renner Wunderlich

1992
Educating Peter produced by: Thomas Goodwin, Gerardine Wurzburg

1991
Deadly Deception: General Electric, Nuclear Weapons and Our Environment
produced by: Debra Chasnoff

1990
Days of Waiting produced by: Steven Okazaki

1989
Johnstown Flood, The produced by: Charles Guggenheim

1988
You Don't Have to Die produced by: Malcolm Clarke, William Guttentag

1987
Young at Heart produced by: Pamela Conn, Sue Marx

1986
Women—For America, for the World produced by: Vivienne Verdon-Roe

1985
Witness to War: Dr. Charlie Clements produced by: David Goodman

1984
Stone Carvers, The produced by: Marjorie Hunt, Paul Wagner

1983
Flamenco at 5:15 produced by: Cynthia Scott, Adam Symansky

1982
If You Love This Planet produced by: Edward Le Lorrain

1981
Close Harmony produced by: Nigel Noble

1980
Karl Hess: Toward Liberty produced by: Roland Hallé, Peter Ladue

1979
Paul Robeson: Tribute to an Artist produced by: Janus

1978
Flight of the Gossamer Condor produced by: Jacqueline Shedd

1977
Gravity Is My Enemy produced by: John Joseph, Jan Stussy

1976
Number Our Days produced by: Lynne Littman

1975
End of the Game, The produced by: Robin Lehman, Claire Wilbur

1974
Don't produced by: Robin Lehman

1973
Princeton: A Search for Answers produced by: Julian Krainin, DeWitt Sage

1972
This Tiny World produced by: Martina Huguenot van der Linden, Charles Huguenot van der Linden

1971
Sentinels of Silence produced by: Robert Amram, Manuel Arango

1970
Interviews with My Lai Veterans produced by: Joseph Strick

1969
Czechoslovakia 1968 produced by: Robert Fresco, Denis Sanders

1968
Why Man Creates produced by: Saul Bass

1967
Redwoods, The produced by: Trevor Greenwood, Mark Harris

1966
Year Toward Tomorrow, A produced by: Edmund Levy

1965
To Be Alive! produced by: Francis Thompson, Inc.

1964
Nine from Little Rock produced by: U.S. Information Agency

1963
Chagall produced by: Simon Schiffrin

1962
Dylan Thomas produced by: Jack Howells

1961
Project Hope produced by: Frank Bibas

1960
Giuseppina produced by: James Hill

1959
Glass produced by: Bert Haanstra

1958
AMA Girls produced by: Ben Sharpsteen

1956
True Story of the Civil War, The produced by: Louis Stoumen

1955
Men Against the Arctic produced by: Walt Disney

1954
Thursday's Children produced by: Morse Films, World Wide Pictures

1953
Alaskan Eskimo, The produced by: Walt Disney

1952
Neighbors produced by: Norman McLaren

1951
Benjy produced by: Fred Zinnemann

1950
Why Korea? produced by: Edmund Reek

1949
Chance to Live, A produced by: Richard de Rochemont
So Much for So Little produced by: Edward Selzer

1948
Toward Independence produced by: U.S. Army

1947
First Steps produced by: United Nations Division of Films and Visual Education

1946
Seeds of Destiny produced by: U.S. War Department

1945
Hitler Lives? produced by: Warner Bros.

1944
With the Marines at Tarawa produced by: U.S. Marine Corp.

1943
December 7th produced by: Field Photographic Branch, Office of Strategic Services, U.S. Navy

SHORT FILM FESTIVALS

The following festivals are either devoted to short films or have a significant short film component.

American Short Shorts Film Festival
www.shortshorts.org

Arcipelago Short Film Festival
www.arcipelagofilmfestival.org

Arizona State University Art Museum Short Film and Video Festival
www.asuartmuseum.asu.edu/filmfest/index.html

Brest Short Film Festival
www.film-festival.brest.com

Brief Encounters Short Film Festival
www.brief-encounters.org.uk

Cannes Film Festival
www.festival-cannes.fr

Cinematexas International Short Film Festival
www.cinematexas.org

Clermont-Ferrand International Short Film Festival
www.clermont-filmfest.com

Crested Butte Reel Fest Short Film Festival
www.crestedbuttereelfest.com

Deauville Festival of American Cinema
www.festival-deauville.com

Film Nite
www.killingtimepictures.com/filmnite

Flickerfest
www.flickerfest.com.au

Girona Film Festival
www.gironafilmfestival.com

Heartland Film Festival
www.heartlandfilmfest.org

Hi Lo Film Festival
www.hilofilmfestival.com

Huesca Film Festival
www.huesca-filmfestival.com

Hull Film
www.hullfilm.co.uk

Interfilm
www.interfilm.de

International Festival of Documentary and Short Film of Bilbao
www.zinebi.com

International Hamburg Short Film
www.shortfilm.com

Jaffas Down the Aisle
www.jaffasdowntheaisle.com.au/launch.htm

Krakow International Documentary and Short Film Festival
www.shortfilm.apollo.pl

Los Angeles Film Festival
www.lafilmfest.com

Los Angeles International Short Film Festival
www.lashortsfest.com

Manhattan Short Film Festival
www.msfilmfest.com

MisFit Short Film Festival
www.ualberta.ca/~filmzone/Misfit/misfit.htm

Montreal International Festival of New Cinema and New Media
www.fcmm.com/2002/en

New York Expo of Short Film and Video
www.nyexpo.org

New York Film Festival
www.filmlinc.com/nyff/nyff.htm

Norwegian Short Film Festival
www.kortfilmfestivalen.no

Rushes Soho Shorts Festival
www.sohoshorts.com

Santa Barbara International Film Festival
www.sbfilmfestival.org

Sao Paulo International Short Film Festival
www.kinoforum.org/curtas/e_index.htm

Shorts Film Festival
www.shortsfilmfestival.com

Shorts International Film Festival
www.shorts.org

Shortspan
www.dreamspan.com/shortspan/index.cfm

Slamdance International Film Festival
www.slamdance.com

South by Southwest
www.sxsw.com

Summer Shorts
www.summershorts.com/index.html

Sundance Film Festival
festival.sundance.org/index.aspx

Tampere International Short Film Festival
www.tamperefilmfestival.fi

Telluride Film Festival
www.telluridefilmfestival.com

Toronto International Film Festival
www.e.bell.ca/filmfest

Uppsala International Short Film Festival
www.shortfilmfestival.com

Valleyfest Film Festival
www.valleyfest.com

Webcuts
www.webcuts.org

Yorkton Short Film and Video Festival
www.yorktonshortfilm.org

Zinebi
www.zinebi.com

SOFTWARE

Adobe Premiere
   www.adobe.com/products/premiere/main.html

After Effects
   www.adobe.com/products/aftereffects/main.html

Final Cut Pro
   www.apple.com/finalcutpro

Maya
   www.aliaswavefront.com/en/products/maya/index.html

THE RIGHT HOOK
by Luke Greenfield & Dave Scotti

FADE IN ON:

INT. BAR — NIGHT
A single man's point-of-view scoping out the crowded bar on a Friday night. We move from beautiful girl to beautiful girl, scanning past all the single men hitting on them. We end on a GUY and GIRL, thoroughly enjoying themselves, as they slowly dance together on the dance floor.

We reveal this has all been from the point-of-view of BRUNO, 30, small and nervous. Bruno stands in the back, observing the social scene. He watches . . .

INT. BAR COUNTER—BAR—NIGHT
A charming guy, TYLER, approaches a beautiful blonde, SEENI, at the bar counter. Tyler has a laughing smile . . .

TYLER: I know I know you from somewhere . . .

Seeni smiles. She's attracted to him. Tyler laughs.

Bruno watches, listening carefully . . .

SEENI: . . . Oh, I see you on the stairmaster.

TYLER (with pride): Stairmaster? No, I only do free-weights.

SEENI: Oh.

TYLER: Yeah. Free-weights.

Bruno watches another "hook-up" in process. A dark-haired guy, CHRIS, smiles intimately with a WOMAN, his face very close to hers.

We notice the COUPLE on the dance floor again. They're dancing closer now, more intimate. He grooves behind her. Bruno looks to his left and sees . . .

INT. BAR COUNTER—BAR—NIGHT
A gorgeous blonde, LISA, leaning back against the bar. MITCH, a cheezy L.A. guy, impresses her.

MITCH: Well, I'm in the industry.

LISA: Oh.

MITCH: Ehh, it's a living (shrugs) What can you do.

Bruno watches as Mitch whispers something in her ear. Lisa smiles and Mitch leads her out of the bar. Bruno watches in disbelief.

Bruno notices the Couple dancing again. Now they're very sensual. His hands slowly run up the sides of her body as they groove together. She bends her neck back as they kiss.

Bruno gets anxious. He scans the bar again. He notices TWO AT-TRACTIVE WOMEN at the counter together. One of them leaves for the bathroom leaving the other alone. This is his chance . . .

INT. BAR COUNTER—BAR—NIGHT
Nervously, Bruno approaches the lone woman, SHAUNA, at the bar. He stops, hesitates, then continues. Suddenly Shauna happens to look over her shoulder and notice him. Bruno freezes and smiles, embarrassed. Shauna double-takes him, then turns back around, thinking he's a freak.

Feeling stupid, Bruno checks to see if anyone noticed this and walks away.

INT. BAR COUNTER—BAR—NIGHT
Bruno stands on the edge of the dance floor, watching two at-tractive girls, MEG and MANDY, dance. With great hesitation, he nonchalantly dances over to them. Making eye contact with the Girls, he smiles and imitates their dance moves.

The Girls smile at each other and politely dance away. Feel-ing self-conscious, Bruno is left dancing alone. Then he turns and notices a vivacious gay guy, CLIVE, has danced up to him. Bruno smiles politely and leaves.

INT. TABLE NEXT TO BAR—NIGHT
Excited and nervous, Bruno sits with a nice woman, TRISH, 30. Bruno's trying hard but the conversation is stale.

 BRUNO (pretends interest): Oh, so you're like a re-ceptionist.

TRISH: Yeah.

BRUNO: Oh, that's cool. Okay. Wow, so you probably get a lot of phone calls and stuff.

TRISH: Yeah. A lot of phone calls.

BRUNO: I mean, is it fun at all? Is there any things you can do at—

CHAD, a suave stud, steps right in front of Bruno. He has complete confidence as he looks down at Trish.

CHAD: Hi . . . I've been watching you from over there and . . .

Bruno struggles, trying to peek around Chad's waist.

CHAD: . . . I really want to take you home right now, and just bang the hell out of you . . . Would that interest you?

Trish looks up at Chad. She breaks a flattered smile, thinks for a moment, then grabs her purse and leaves with him.

Bruno, mouth agape, watches in disbelief. He bows his head.

FADE OUT

INT. BAR COUNTER—BAR—NIGHT
DANNY, warm and attractive, stands with Bruno at the bar. They're buying beers.

BRUNO (dead serious): Dan, I gotta ask you something. And you gotta be dead honest with me, alright?

DANNY: Yeah.

BRUNO: . . . Am I ugly?

They stare at each other. Danny hesitates.

DANNY: . . . No.

BRUNO (relieved sigh): I mean, I don't know what it is, man. I'm so . . . <u>nervous</u> to go up to chicks lately. You know? . . . I feel like such a dickhead. (subtle look around) I mean, am I a dickhead?

DANNY (amused light laugh): No . . . Don't worry about it. You just gotta get comfortable, you know?

BRUNO (tired, discouraged): But <u>how</u>? You know? They <u>know.</u> They <u>know</u> what I want. I feel like such an id-iot. "Hey, you look familiar." (scoffs) I mean, they <u>know.</u> (motions to his face) They <u>know</u> I'm not famil-iar.

DANNY: No, you need a way in, you know? A hook.

BRUNO: Whatdya mean, a hook?

DANNY (trying to explain): Something different. You know? Something you can do that gets you in, gets you comfortable . . . Makes you <u>both</u> comfortable.

BRUNO (to himself): Fuck, I need that.

DANNY: Yeah, you gotta break the awkwardness so you can talk.

Bruno's POV of Two Girls talking. Bruno thinks . . .

BRUNO: A hook. Yeah, that's great . . . Well, what's your hook?

DANNY: Well, I don't need one.

BRUNO (agreeing): Yeah, that's true. (small beat) Fuck, what should my hook be?

DANNY: You just gotta be yourself.

BRUNO: No, no, no, that doesn't work. I hate bein' myself.

DANNY (light laugh): Brune, you got a great personality, man. You got some great qualities. Use them.

BRUNO: . . . Well, like what qualities?

Danny pauses. He can think of nothing. He looks up at Bruno.

BRUNO: . . . It's alright. Don't worry about it.

DANNY: But you see what I'm saying—

BRUNO: Yeah, yeah.

DANNY: I mean no one can tell you what your hook is. You just gotta find it, man. It'll come . . . It'll come.

Pause. Bruno thinks.

BRUNO: Dan, it better, man, cause I'm telling ya. I need a girlfriend. I mean I gotta fuck something. Anything. I'll fuck anything. Guy or girl, it doesn't even matter anymore.

Bruno follows Danny's gaze to the BAR OWNER standing on the other side of the bar. Repulsed, the Bar Owner walks away.

DANNY: That was good.

BRUNO (waves it off): Look, do me a favor. Don't tell the guys I asked you about this kind of stuff.

Danny grabs his beer and turns to head for their table.

DANNY: Who am I gonna tell? <u>Gary</u>?

INT. TABLE—BAR—NIGHT

Bruno and Danny sit at the other side of the table from GARY, 30. Gary is their wise-ass, childhood friend. Gary's side-kicks sit on either side of him. On the left is FREDDY, a funny-looking guy who's not so bright. JAKE is on the right.

Jake laughs wildly with Gary.

GARY (to Jake): Alright, relax, relax. (to Bruno) Look, you wanna get the ladies, Brune? Huh? A little advice.

DANNY (smiles, sarcastic) Here we go.

Bruno exchanges a look with Danny. Off Danny's gaze, Bruno notices a CUTE BRUNETTE sit down alone at the bar.

BRUNO: Gar, please—

GARY: Here's the key to women. You just degrade the fuck out of them and make 'em feel like shit.

BRUNO: That's brilliant, Gary. Thank you. I appreci-ate the advice.

GARY: Just watch this. You just walk up to her and go . . . (turns to Freddy) "Hi, are you okay? Is everything alright?"

Jake laughs. Bruno exchanges a look with Danny.

Gary turns back to Bruno and points at him.

GARY: Or try this one . . .

SMASH CUT TO:

INT. BAR COUNTER—BAR—NIGHT
Gary walks up to KATE, an attractive woman at the bar.

Gary (V.O.): Excuse me. I'm sorry, are you okay?

The Woman turns, looking worried and self-conscious. She touches her right cheek.

BACK TO:

INT. TABLE—BAR—NIGHT
Gary smiles with excitement.

GARY: Boom. You see, you got her now. She's self-conscious, she's worried. She feels like there's something wrong with her. (pause) Now you're in control. (stares at Bruno) And now you have the power.

Pause. Bruno and Danny stare at Gary. Then they exchange looks.

BRUNO: You need a psychiatrist, Gar.

Appendix V

GARY: Alright, Brune.

DANNY: Sounds like you got some issues there, Gar.

GARY: Hey, Dan. You don't need the advice. We all know that. But Bruno, seriously, with your looks, I'd be taking all the advice I could get.

Jake laughs lightly.

BRUNO: You got a mirror in your house, Gar? Huh? Get your mom to put a mirror in your room.

Jake, Freddy, and Dan laugh. Gary goes along with it.

GARY: Hey, better lookin' than you, pal.

BRUNO (sarcastic): Yeah.

GARY (smiling like "I am"): <u>Yeah.</u>

BRUNO: . . . You're better lookin' than me?

GARY: Yeah.

BRUNO (in disbelief): . . . You think you're better lookin' than I am?

GARY: Bruno. A lot better.

Pause. Bruno and Gary stare at each other. Bruno suddenly turns to Danny.

BRUNO: Dan, seriously, who's better—?

DANNY: Oh, fuck that.

BRUNO: No, seriously. Seriously, who?

DANNY: Jesus! No.

GARY: Bruno, Bruno, you're makin' it worse for your-self. Look, you wanna stay a virgin, stay a virgin. What do I care?

BRUNO (scoffs): A virgin . . . Do you know how many fuckin' chicks I've had?

GARY: . . . How many?

BRUNO: . . . I'm not gonna—What? I'm gonna count em up for you right now—

GARY: How many?

BRUNO: —No. I'm not gonna sit here and name you all the girls I've <u>had.</u>

GARY: Bruno, how many—

BRUNO: <u>A lot.</u> A lot. More than I can count.

GARY (laughing): Bruno, name one. Just name one.

BRUNO: I nailed Chrissy Abatello in eighth grade.

This causes an uproar at the table.

EVERYONE: Bullshit! Right! Chrissy Abatello. <u>When? When?</u>

BRUNO: . . . When. March 6th, 1983. What'd I fuckin' write it down? . . . You know, what is this? I don't have to prove myself to you guys. This is bullshit—

GARY: Hey-hey-hey, what are you getting so upset about? . . . (almost sincere) What'd you fall in love with her?

BRUNO: . . . You know how many years it took me to get over that? . . . You know, that's exactly the kind of thing—You know what? I'm not even gonna talk to you about it. It's too complicated for you guys . . . Why am I even wasting my time here, when I could be over there getting laid right now.

Gary, perplexed, looks over at the bar.

GARY: By who? The bartender?

Everyone roars.

BRUNO (looking at Brunette): Right there.

GARY ("are you serious?"): The girl at the bar?

BRUNO: Yeah.

GARY: . . . The brunette.

BRUNO: Yes, Gary. The girl.

Pause. Gary's getting excited. He can't believe Bruno's serious. He stands up, reaches into his pocket and drops a big wad of bills on the table.

GARY: Bruno? Right now. Three hundred dollars. Let's go.

Everyone laughs.

BRUNO: Good. I could use the money.

GARY: Good. Let's go. Let's see it.

DANNY: Alright, guys. Let's just relax.

GARY: No, no, no, he dug his own grave here. Bruno, let's go. I want to see this.

BRUNO: Fine. You know what? I'm gonna go over there, take her home, and while I'm <u>fucking</u> her, I'm gonna call you on the phone. So make sure your mother don't answer.

GARY (laughing, excited): Hey, Brune. Call collect.

Gary, Jake and Freddy laugh. Bruno turns around and looks off toward the WOMAN sitting at the bar. He lets out a worried sigh. Danny takes notice.

DANNY (softly): Hey, just don't take it too seriously, right? Just have fun with it.

BRUNO (sarcastic): Yeah.

Bruno sighs and is about to walk over . . .

DANNY: Hey . . . what's the worst that can happen?

Bruno takes a deep breath and starts his brave walk to the bar counter.

BRUNO (to himself): I'll be lucky if she spits on me.

INT. BAR COUNTER—BAR—NIGHT
Bruno walks nervously up to ANGELA, the Brunette at the bar.

BRUNO: How ya doin'?

ANGEL (dismissing him): I'm gay.

She looks away. This momentarily throws Bruno. He turns to go back but stops upon seeing the guys. Gary grins, knowing he's won. Danny silently encourages him.

Bruno quickly regains his composure.

    BRUNO: Like a <u>happy</u> gay or . . .

    ANGELA: I'm a lesbian.

Bruno hesitates, then leans in toward her.

    BRUNO: Look, I just came over here to be friendly, you know? I mean, if you're gonna blow me off, fine. But at least be honest about it. Tell me I'm disgusting or ugly or something, but don't tell me you're a <u>lesbian.</u> Cause you are no lesbian. (light laugh) I mean, c'mon . . .

Finding this strange, Angela looks at him. He continues . . .

    BRUNO: I mean, you're not some short-haired . . . fat, angry bull dyke like . . .

He notices Angela's look to someone behind him. Bruno looks over his shoulder to find a large angry woman, CLAIRE, has come up behind him.

    BRUNO (indicating Angry Woman): . . . like that.

Claire is her lover.

Bruno turns and smiles at her.

BRUNO: How ya doin'?

Claire grabs Bruno and BELTS him in the mouth, sending him
to the floor.

Everyone in the bar turns to watch.

Bruno's friends ROAR WITH LAUGHTER!!

INT. BAR FLOOR NEXT TO BAR COUNTER—NIGHT

Danny comes running up to the scene.

DANNY: Whoa, whoa. What happened here? Jesus Christ.

BRUNO (stunned): What the fuck was that?

CLAIRE: You like that? Huh? You want some more?

BRUNO: It was a joke, you fuckin' barbarian!

DANNY: Alright, Brune, relax. Relax. (to Bouncer)
It's alright, it's alright. I got it. I got it.

CLAIRE: Yeah, you're real tough now. Come over here—
Come over here and say it to my face. Huh? C'mon, you
ugly little faggot. I'll give you another beating.

BRUNO: You know, you're disgusting, you know that?

CLAIRE (mocking, like a "pussy"): Meeooow.

Bruno is bewildered.

BRUNO: What _is_ that?! (to Danny) What the fuck is—(to
Claire) You're a fuckin' animal, you know that?

CLAIRE: C'mon, bring it on. Bring it on, you little <u>pussy</u>!

Bruno gets riled up. He paces <u>behind</u> Danny.

BRUNO: <u>What?!</u> I'll kick your ass right now! I'm serious!

Danny's had enough. He calms Bruno.

DANNY: Alright, relax! Relax, okay? Just chill out.

CLAIRE: Then bring it on then. C'mon! Do it.

Bruno stands, embarrassed. Danny walks over to Claire. He can't help but smile at the situation.

DANNY: Hey, what are you doing? Don't egg him on. Alright? You got him. You hurt his feelings. You won. Okay?

Suddenly from behind, Bruno charges and TACKLES Claire, pile-driving her to the floor. Bruno's friends SCREAM with laughter!

Bruno and Claire wrestle wildly on the floor, punching and rolling on top of each other. It's an even match.

Angela watches in shock.

Danny tries to break it up.

DANNY: Alright, Brune. Bruno, c'mon!

INT. END OF BAR COUNTER—NIGHT
A GIGANTIC BOUNCER is about to step in but the OWNER OF THE
BAR doesn't want him to.

    BAR OWNER (sinister smile): Na, na, na. You kidding
    me? Don't touch this.

INT. TABLE—BAR—NIGHT
Gary, Freddy, and Jake laughing and placing bets.

    GARY: Alright, who you got? I got Bruno.

    JAKE: I got Xena.

INT. BAR FLOOR—NIGHT
Bruno and Claire grope each other's faces. Their expressions
SMUSH against each other as they strain.

INT. TABLE—BAR—NIGHT
Gary watches, laughing . . .

    GARY: Atta boy, Brune! Give her the tongue!

INT. BAR FLOOR—NIGHT
Danny continues to break it up.

    DANNY: Hey, alright, enough!

He gets kicked and punched. Finally . . .

    DANNY: Fuck it. Kill each other.

Claire now standing, yanks at Bruno's leg. Bruno spastically
tries to get loose.

BRUNO: Get off! Get the fuck off me!

DANNY (shakes his head): Oh, this looks good.

Claire takes Bruno by the leg and HURLS him like a log into the bottoms of bar stools. Bruno jumps up and rages toward her.

BAM! BAM! Claire CLOCKS him with a combination punch.

INT. TABLE—BAR—NIGHT
Gary, Freddy, and Jake react. Gary grabs his money . . .

GARY: Fuck it. I got the chick.

INT. BAR FLOOR—NIGHT
Bruno tries to escape Claire's vicious attack. He turns to see Danny.

BRUNO (worried): "What's the worst that can happen?!"
You son-of-a-bitch.

Claire yanks Bruno back by his shirt. Bruno grabs her hair, punching wildly. It's chaotic, messy.

They forcefully spin around the room. Bruno thrusts her forward as they FLIP OVER a table. The table going down with them.

A BUSINESSMAN sips his martini as he watches.

INT. END OF BAR COUNTER—NIGHT
The Bar Owner is now jotting down damage costs.

BAR OWNER: One-fifty.

INT. BAR FLOOR BY POOL TABLE—NIGHT

Claire grabs a pool stick away from a big guy, JOHN. Swing-
ing it like an axe at Bruno, she SHATTERS a lamp!

INT. END OF BAR COUNTER—NIGHT

The Bar Owner writes it down.

    BAR OWNER (jotting it down): Three hundred.

INT. BAR FLOOR BY POOL TABLE—NIGHT

Claire SWINGS wildly and accidentally WHACKS a Cocktail
Waitress in the lower back! Screaming, she falls forward!

INT. TABLE—BAR—NIGHT

Gary laughs hysterically, watching the fight.

INT. BAR FLOOR BY POOL TABLE—NIGHT

Bruno gets up. He grabs a CUE BALL off the pool table and
WHIPS it at Claire. She ducks . . .

INT. TABLE—BAR—NIGHT

WHACK! It SMACKS Gary in the face. Down he goes, holding his
face.

INT. BAR FLOOR—NIGHT

Claire SMASHES a bottle across Bruno's head!

Angela watches in disgust.

Bruno FLIPS Claire on her back SMASHING HER onto a table of
bottles.

Danny cringes.

INT. END OF BAR COUNTER—NIGHT
The Bar Owner and Bouncer react.

INT. BAR FLOOR—NIGHT
Claire grabs Bruno, charges toward a large glass trophy case, and FLIPS HIM over her shoulder. CRASH! Bruno's back SHATTERS through the glass case as he's head-over-heels. They both fall to the ground in a rain of broken glass.

INT. BAR COUNTER—BAR—NIGHT
Angela has had enough. She grabs her purse.

INT. BAR FLOOR—NIGHT
Beaten, bloodied, and completely out of breath, Bruno and Claire lie still, holding each other at arms length by their necks.

They notice Angela angrily leave the bar. Bruno and Claire gaze at each other for a moment.

Pause.

   BRUNO (out of breath): Can't I just buy you a drink?

   CLAIRE: . . . All you had to do was ask.

They release their death grips. They look at each other. Pause. They kiss.

                                          FADE OUT

INT. TABLE—BAR—NIGHT
All five guys sit around the table again. Bruno exudes a new confidence now as he relaxes back in his chair. Gary sits next to him wearing a nose cast.

A COCKTAIL WAITRESS places a full beer in front of Bruno.

    COCKTAIL WAITRESS: Here you go, Brune.

    BRUNO: Thanks, hon.

A young, attractive woman, STACEY, walks by.

    STACEY: Hi Bruno.

    BRUNO (casually): Hey.

    GARY: What the fuck is this? What are you, Mickey Rourke now?

    BRUNO (shrugs modestly): Hey, I got it now. I found my hook.

Bruno gives a knowing look to Danny.

    GARY: A hook? What the fuck does <u>that</u> mean?

Bruno watches an ATTRACTIVE WOMAN take a seat at the bar.

    BRUNO: Well . . . (slowly gets up) Watch and learn, Gar. Watch and learn.

INT. BAR COUNTER—BAR—NIGHT
Bruno casually walks up to STEPHANIE, the Attractive Woman at the bar. He smiles confidently.

    BRUNO: So, how we doin' tonight?

She looks him up and down. Then scoffs . . .

STEPHANIE: Get the fuck away from me, loser.

Bruno looks away, thinks for a moment.

Suddenly, he CRACKS her jaw with the right hook!

1ST TITLE
Bruno TACKLES her and PILE-DRIVES her into the CAMERA.

2ND TITLE
Stephanie slowly gets up and rips off her jacket . . .

STEPHANIE: Alright, bitch. You want some of this?

She gets into a Kung-Fu stance. Shocked, Bruno takes a step
back as she delivers a devastating SPIN-KICK to his head.

3RD TITLE
Bruno helplessly blocks the onslaught of punches and kicks.

BRUNO: No, no, no. I'm just trying to—(lowers his
guard) Can't I just buy you a drink?

POW! She CRACKS him with a powerful punch in the face.

4TH TITLE
Bruno's friends wince and cringe as Bruno gets his beating.

ENDING TITLES

DAUGHTER
final draft by Eduardo Rodriguez
written by Eduardo Rodriguez
February 27, 2001

INT. SHAE'S BEDROOM—NIGHTMARE

SHAE POWELL, a gorgeous brunette in her late twenties, sleeps in her bed. She gets out of her bed and approaches the door.

As she grabs for the knob, the knob falls off of the door and blood gushes from where the knob had been. Suddenly, a child's hand bursts through the hole and grabs Shae's arm.

    SOPHIE (V.O.): There are no doors. How can you leave
    if there are no doors?

BLOOD POURS OVER CAMERA . . .

INT. SHAE'S BEDROOM—NIGHT

Shae screams and opens her eyes. She sits, soaked in sweat, and looks around. Expensive paintings on the wall are her only company.

Shae stares at her hands. The silver crucifix that hangs from a small chain on her left wrist shakes frantically. Shae scoots forward to the foot of the bed.

She gets out of bed wearing a black bikini bottom with matching tank top and walks barefoot towards . . .

INT. SOPHIE'S ROOM—CONTINUOUS

Shae opens the door carefully. SOPHIE POWELL, her five year old, blonde-haired daughter is on her bed, is completely covered by a thick, colorful blanket. Shae frowns and approaches the bed.

Shae pulls the blanket off of Sophie's head and kisses her forehead. Sophie seems to be completely asleep and is holding her favorite doll. Shae closes the door slowly, making sure that she won't wake her daughter. As soon as Shae closes the door, Sophie opens her eyes.

SOPHIE STARES STRAIGHT AT CAMERA.

INT. KITCHEN—CONTINUOUS
Shae walks in, grabs a glass and fills it at the sink. As she is about to drink, she sees what appears to be blood coming from the bottom of the fridge door.

Shae approaches the fridge and gets on her knees. Shae stares at the stain puzzled. She starts opening the door very slowly. She leans forward to take a cautious peek. The fridge door is almost completely open when something seems to jump out at her.

Shae grasps and backs up. She looks down. A bottle of strawberry syrup without its cap lies over the stain of red liquid. She puts her hand on her chest and breathes deeply.

     SHAE (disapprovingly): Sophie.

Suddenly a door slams. She's startled. Silence. Shae takes a peek down the hallway . . .

INT. HALLWAY—CONTINUOUS
The light in her bedroom is now on.

    SHAE: Sophie, honey are you up?

Silence. Shae walks to . . .

INT. BEDROOM—CONTINUOUS
Shae walks to the doorway and looks around . . . Sophie is not
there. Shae is confused. Suddenly, the bathtub's faucet turns
on. Shae turns around and walks to . . .

INT. IN FRONT OF BATHROOM DOOR—CONTINUOUS
Shae tries to open the door but it's locked.

    SHAE: Sophie?

No answer.

    SHAE (CONT'D): Answer me.

Silence.

    SHAE (CONT'D): Sophie Powell open the door immedi-
    ately!

She tries again. The door doesn't move an inch. She tries one
more time. Nothing.

    SHAE (CONT'D): SOPHIE!

She takes a deep breath and starts turning around.

    SHAE (CONT'D): Honey stop playing games with me.
    I . . .

Shae stares at her reflection in the mirror. The bathroom door behind her is now completely OPEN. She turns around. The door is still open. The bathtub's faucet turns off. Silence. She stares at the darkness, hoping that Sophie is in there.

SHAE (CONT'D): Sweetie it's too late for these games.

Silence.

SHAE (CONT'D): You're scaring Mom.

Shae searches for the light switch with her right hand. The silver cross on her wrist is devoured by the darkness. Shae finds the light switch and flips it. Nothing. She flips the light switch again. Darkness . . .

Shae slowly starts sticking her head into the darkness of the bathroom. Shae squints to sharpen her sight in the darkness.

SHAE (CONT'D): Sophie?

Suddenly, Shae screams and falls back. She grabs her foot and looks at it. A razor blade is stuck in her foot. She pulls out the blade and screams again.

FLASH TO:

HALLUCINATION
Shae hums "Hush Little Mockingbird" while she sits on a mattress soaked in blood and covered with worms.

Sophie stands inside a bathtub filled with a white substance, holding her doll. SHE STARES STRAIGHT AT CAMERA.

Shae's hand against a white wall.

Sophie lies in a fetal position on a red ceiling.

SHAE FACES CAMERA WITH HER EYES CLOSED. She opens them to reveal her white eyes.

Shae's lips kiss Sophie on her forehead.

Blood flows out from underneath a door.

INT. BEDROOM—CONTINUOUS
Shae is horrified. She tosses the razor blade and crawls back
to her bed.

She grabs a white sock off of the floor, next to her tennis
shoes. She dabs her wound with the sock and notices that her
hands are trembling. Shae sees that her bracelet is not on
her wrist anymore.

Suddenly the mirror starts bleeding behind her and she sees
it. Shae screams and backs out of the room.

INT. HALLWAY—CONTINUOUS
Shae stares at her room. She looks back at Sophie's room and
runs through the hallways towards . . .

INT. SOPHIE'S ROOM—CONTINUOUS
Shae opens the door. Sophie is still in her bed. Shae rushes
in and pulls the blanket. Shae stares at the mattress . . .

. . . there is no Sophie. A white doll lies on the bloodied
bed. Worms wiggle all over the bed.

                                            FLASH TO:

HALLUCINATION

Shae hums "Hush Little Mockingbird" while she tries to stop the gushing blood sweeping from the hole where the door knob was.

Shae lies on a red ceiling in a fetal position.

A bloodied footprint on a white floor.

SHAE FACES CAMERA. Her white eyes are wide open and she is screaming her lungs out.

Sophie smiles.

Shae stands inside a bathtub filled with a white substance, holding Sophie's doll. SHE STARES STRAIGHT AT CAMERA.

A torrent of blood comes gushing under the door.

INT. SOPHIE'S ROOM—CONTINUOUS
Shae falls to her knees. Suddenly, Shae sees what seems to be Sophie running towards her room.

    SHAE: Sophie, stop!

Shae rushes out of the room. The door slams behind her.

INT. HALLWAY—CONTINUOUS
Shae runs through the hallway . . .

INT. BEDROOM—CONTINUOUS
Shae rushes in and stops on the spot, looking straight ahead. Slowly, she turns her head towards the bathroom. Now, the door is open and the light is on. Shae is completely stunned.

Shae walks into . . .

INT. BATHROOM—CONTINUOUS

Shae enters and looks up. The ceiling is completely red. She can't believe what she is seeing. Shae looks at the vanity to see that the mirror and sink have turned entirely white. The whole bathroom has become a white temple.

Suddenly Shae hears Sophie humming "Hush Little Mockingbird" behind the tub's curtain. She starts walking towards the bathtub, slowly, very slowly. She stops in front of the curtain.

She pulls the curtain and no one is there. Silence. Shae sees her silver bracelet in the bottom of the bathtub. She kneels down to reach for the crucifix . . .

SPLASH, a doll falls from the ceiling into the bathtub and bleeds, turning the water red. Shae screams.

Shae looks at the bathtub and starts crying. She is shocked. Suddenly the door of the bathroom slams shut. Shae turns around and leans her back against the tub. Sophie faces Shae.

SOPHIE: They said that you have to stay here, Mommy.

Shae starts bawling. Sophie stares at Shae.

SHAE (crying): Why do I have to stay here?

Sophie starts walking towards Shae.

SOPHIE: There are no doors. How can you leave if there are no doors?

Sophie stands in front of her mom. Silence.

SHAE: Sophie, please no. In the name of God . . .

Sophie leans forward, getting very close to Shae's ear.

SOPHIE: God has nothing to do with this, Mommy.

Shae closes her eyes.

FLASH TO:

FLASHBACK
Shae cuts Sophie's wrist.

Blood and water spill over the edge of the tub onto Sophie's doll.

Shae cuts her own wrist.

The crucifix falls into the bathtub. Blood drips into the water.

Shae and Sophie lie in the bathtub. Blood fills the bathtub.

The bathroom door closes.

Blood gushes out under the door.

INT. BATHROOM—CONTINUOUS
Shae cries desperately. She turns around . . .

SHAE: Sophie, please forgive me . . .

The bathroom door turns a white indentation with no texture . . .

INT. WHITE ROOM—CONTINUOUS

Shae screams her lungs out. Her eyes are completely white. Shae is alone and soaked in blood. She gets on her feet and walks towards the door, leaving red footprints behind her.

Shae approaches the door and reaches for the knob . . . nothing. It's not even a door. Just an outlined rectangle on the wall. Slowly it fades.

> SOPHIE (V.O.): There are no doors. How can you leave if there are no doors?

Shae falls to her knees. She lies there, against the white wall.

> SOPHIE (CONT'D): They don't have doors in Hell.

Shae stares at the red ceiling of the room . . .

DISSOLVE TO:

EXT. HELL—CONTINUOUS
A white cube with a red ceiling floats in the middle of nowhere. We hear Shae humming "Hush Little Mockingbird."

PULL BACK TO REVEAL:

Dozens of cubes float in nothingness. Each one of them with a different colored ceiling. Each with its own specific sound.

FADE TO BLACK.

THE END

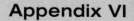

Appendix VI

COMPLETE SHORT-FILM BUDGET

Quality Filmed Entertainment
INSIDE

Bid date: 5/14/01

Production Co.:	**Quality Filmed Entertainment**
Address:	5478 WILSHIRE BLVD
	LOS ANGELES CA
Telephone:	323.939.7274
Fax:	323.939.6836
Job #:	
Contract:	Steve Hein/Gary Bryman
Director:	Trevor Sands
Producer:	Gary Bryman, Steve Hein
DP:	Eric Haase
Art Director:	Paul Macherey
Editor:	Trevor Sands
Pre-Production Days:	7
Build & Strike Days:	3 Hours: 12
Pre-Light Days:	Hours: 12
Studio Shoot Days:	2 Hours: 14
Location Days:	1 Hours: 12
Location(s):	Padded Cell

SUMMARY OF ESTIMATED PRODUCTION COSTS		ESTIMATED	ACTUAL	VARIANCE
1 Pre-production & Wrap Costs	Totals A & C	3,367	1,384.69	(1,982.31)
2 Shooting Labor	Total B	4,849	7,778.00	2,929.00
3 Location & Travel Expenses	Total D	3,930	4,098.70	168.70
4 Props, Wardrobe & Animals	Total E	560	358.00	(202.00)
5 Studio & Set Construction Costs	Total F, G & H	3,500	6,130.15	2,630.15
6 Equipment Costs	Total I	6,520	8,873.90	2,353.90
7 Filmstock, Process & Print	Total J	5,400	8,501.18	3,101.18
8 Miscellaneous	Total K	500	1,700.00	1,200.00
9	**Subtotal A to K**	28,626	38,824.62	10,198.62
10 Director /Creative Fees (not included in Direct Costs)	Total L			
11 Insurance				
12	**Subtotal Direct Costs**	28,626	38,824.62	10,198.62
13 Production Fee				
14 Talent Labor & expenses	Totals M & N			
15 Editorial & Finishing	Totals O & P	2,000	4,349.50	2,349.50
16				
17 Other				
18 Other				
19				

Contracted Total	30,626	**GRAND TOTAL**	
Contingency Day			

GRAND TOTAL	ESTIMATED	ACTUAL	VARIANCE
	$30,626	$43,174.12	$12,548.12

COMMENTS

1 Prep Day
3 12 Hour Days
1 Wrap day

	PRE-PRO & WRAP			OT Hours			
A	CREW	Days	Rate	1.5	2.0	ESTIMATED	ACTUAL
1	Producer						
2	Assistant Director						
3	Director of Photography						
4	Camera Operator						
5	Assistant Camera	1	50			50	
6	Production Designer	10	50			500	
7	Prop Assistant	5	50			250	
8	Inside Prop	5	50			250	
9							
10							
11	Electrician	2	50			100	
12	Best Boy Electrician	2	50			100	
13	3rd Electrician						
14	4th Electrician						
15							
16	Grip	2	50			100	

A	**PRE-PRO & WRAP** **CREW**	Days	Rate	OT Hours 1.5	2.0	**ESTIMATED**	**ACTUAL**
17	2nd Grip	2	50			100	
18	3rd Grip						
19	4th Grip						
20	Mixer						
21	Boom						
22	Recordist						
23	Playback						
24	Makeup Artist						
25	Hair Stylist						
26	Wardrobe Stylist						
27	Wardrobe Attendant						
28	Script Supervisor						
29	Home Economist						
30	2nd Home Economist						
31	VTR Operator						
32	EFX Foreman						
33	Scenic						
34	Teleprompter Operator						
35	Generator Operator						
36	Still Photographer						
37	Location Scout						
38	Script Supervisor						
39	Production Coordinator						
40	Nurse						
41	Craft Service	1	50			50	
42	Fire Safety Officers						
43	Policemen						
44	Welfare Worker/Teacher						
45	Teamster						
46	2nd Teamster						
47	2nd Assistant Director						
48	Production Assistants						
49	Production Assistants						
50							
		30		**Sub-total A**		1,500	
				PT/P&W		317	
				TOTAL A		1,817	

B	**SHOOTING** **CREW**	Days	Rate	OT Hours 1.5	2.0	**ESTIMATED**	**ACTUAL**
51	Producer						
52	Assistant Director	6	50			300	300.00
53	Director of Photography						
54	Camera Operator						250.00
55	Assistant Camera	3	50			150	800.00
56	Production Designer	3	50			150	500.00

B	SHOOTING CREW	Days	Rate	OT Hours 1.5	OT Hours 2.0	ESTIMATED	ACTUAL
57	Prop Assistant	3	50			150	
58	Inside Prop	3	50			150	
59							
60							
61	Electrician	3	50			150	450.00
62	Best Boy Electrician	3	50			150	400.00
63	3rd Electrician	3	50			150	175.00
64	4th Electrician	3	50			150	400.00
65							
66	Grip	3	50			150	450.00
67	2nd Grip	3	50			150	150.00
68	3rd Grip	3	50			150	200.00
69	4th Grip	3	50			150	600.00
70	Mixer	3	300			900	1,800.00
71	Boom	3	50			150	
72	Recordist						
73	Playback						
74	Makeup Artist	3	50			150	250.00
75	Hair Stylist						
76	Wardrobe Stylist	3	50			150	200.00
77	Wardrobe Attendant						100.00
78	Script Supervisor	3	50			150	153.00
79	Home Economist						
80	2nd Home Economist						
81	VTR Operator						
82	EFX Foreman						
83	Scenic						
84	Teleprompter Operator						
85	Generator Operator						
86	Still Photographer						
87	Location Scout						
88	Production Manager						
89	Production Coordinator						
90	Nurse						
91	Craft Service	3	50			150	600.00
92	Fire Safety Officers						
93	Policeman						
94	Welfare Worker / Teacher	1	250			250	
95	Teamster						
96	2nd Teamster						
97	2nd Assistant Director						
98	Production Assistants						
99	Production Assistants						
100							
		61			Sub-total B	4,000	7,778.00
					PT/P&W	849	
					TOTAL B	4,849	7,778.00

C	PRE-PRODUCTION & WRAP EXPENSES	Amount	Rate	X	ESTIMATED	ACTUAL
101	Auto Rentals					
102	Air Fares					
103	Per Diems					
104	Still Camera Rental & Film					
105	Messengers					
106	Trucking	5	90	2	900	680.32
107	Deliveries and Taxis					
108	Home Economist Supplies					
109	Telephone and Cable					
110	Casting Director	1	500		500	500.00
111	Casting Facilities					
112	Working Meals	1	150		150	204.37
113						
				TOTAL C	1,550	1384.69

D	LOCATION AND TRAVEL EXPENSES	Amount	Rate	X	ESTIMATED	ACTUAL
114	Location Fees	1	500		500	
115	Permits	1	490		490	1,213.00
116	Car Rentals					
117	Bus Rentals					
118	Dressing Room Vehicles					
119	Parking, Tolls, and Gas					382.39
120	Trucking					
121	Other Vehicles					
122	Other Vehicles					
123	Customs					
124	Excess Bags					
125	Air Fares					
126	Per Diems					
127	Air Fares					
128	Per Diems					
129	Breakfast	3	8	30	720	
130	Lunch	3	8	30	720	1,562.65
131	Dinner	3	10	30	900	178.97
132	Set Security					
133	Limousines					
134	Other Transportation					
135	Kit Rentals	2	50	3	300	
136	Art Work					
137	Gratuities					
138	Craft Services	3	100		300	761.69
139						
				TOTAL D	3,930	4,098.70

E	PROPS, WARDROBE & ANIMALS	Amount	Rate	X	ESTIMATED	ACTUAL
140	Prop Rentals					108.00
141	Prop Purchases					
142	Wardrobe Rentals	8	50	1	400	250.00
143	Wardrobe Purchases	8	20		160	
144	Picture Vehicles					
145	Animals and Handlers					
146	Makeup EFX, Wigs Etc.					
147	Product Color Correction					
148						
149						
150						
	TOTAL E				560	358.00

F	STUDIO RENTAL & EXPENSES	Amount	Rate	X	ESTIMATED	ACTUAL
151	Rental For Build Days	3	300		900	
152	Build OT Hours					
153	Rental for Pre-Lite Days					
154	Pre-Lite OT Hours					
155	Rental for Shoot Days	2	500		1,000	2,500.00
156	Shoot OT Hours					
157	Rental for Strike Days					
158	Strike OT Hours					
159	Generator and Operator					
160	Studio Security					
161	Power Charges and Bulbs	12	25	2	600	
162	Studio Related					
163	Meals for Crew and Talent					
164	Stage Manager					
165						
166						
167						
	TOTAL F				2,500	2,500.00

G	SET CONSTRUCTION CREW	Days	Rate	OT Hours 1.5	OT Hours 2.0	ESTIMATED	ACTUAL
168	Set Designer						
169	Carpenters						
170	Grips						
171	Outside Props						
172	Inside Props						
173	Scenics						
174	Electricians						
175	Teamsters						
176	Strike Labor						
177	Art PA's						
178	Art PA's						

G	SET CONSTRUCTION CREW	Days	Rate	OT Hours 1.5	2.0	ESTIMATED	ACTUAL
179							
180							
				Sub-total G			
				PT/P&W			
				TOTAL G			

H	SET CONSTRUCTION MATERIALS	Amount	Rate	X	ESTIMATED	ACTUAL
181	Set Dressing Rentals					1,605.15
182	Set Dressing Purchases					1,500.00
183	Lumber	1	500		500	
184	Paint	1	250		250	
185	Hardware	1	250		250	525.00
186	Special Effects					
187	Outside Construction					
188	Trucking					
189	Messengers and Deliveries					
190	Kit Rentals					
191						
192						
	TOTAL H				1,000	3,630.15

I	EQUIPMENT COSTS	Amount	Rate	X	ESTIMATED	ACTUAL
193	Camera Rental	1	1500		1,500	1,800.00
194	Sound Rental	3	90		270	1,312.75
195	Lighting Rental	3	650		1,950	
196	Grip Rental	3	350		1,050	2,799.78
197	Generator Rental	1	400		400	
198	Crane Rental					
199	VTR Rental					
200	Walkie Talkie Rental	10	10	2	200	200.00
201	Dolly Rental	1	450		450	366.12
202	Camera Car Rental					
203	Camera Aircraft Rental					
204	Production Supplies	1	250		250	756.99
205	Teleprompter					
206	Crane Rental					1,225.26
207	L & D	1	250		250	
208	Grip Expendable	1	100		100	90.00
209	Lighting Expendable	1	100		100	50.00
210	Turn Table					273.00
	TOTAL I				6,520	8,873.90

J	FILMSTOCK, PROCESS & PRINT	Amount	Rate	X	ESTIMATED	ACTUAL
211	Purchase Filmstock	12000	0.31		3,720	8,501.18
212	Process Filmstock	12000	0.14		1,680	
213	Print Filmstock					
214	Transfer to Mag.					
215	Sync & Screen Dailies					
216						
				TOTAL J	5,400	8,501.18

K	MISCELLANEOUS EXPENSES	Amount	Rate	X	ESTIMATED	ACTUAL
217	Petty Cash					
218	Air Shipping and Carriers					
219	Phones and Cables					
220						
221	External Billing Costs					
222	Special Insurance	1	500		500	1,700.00
223						
224						
225						
226						
				TOTAL K	500	1,700.00

L	DIRECTOR/CREATIVE FEES	Amount	Rate	X	ESTIMATED	ACTUAL
227	Director Prep					
228	Director Travel					
229	Director Shoot					
230	Director Post					
231						
232						
233						
				Sub-total L		
				PT/P&W		
				TOTAL L		

| | TALENT | | Travel | Shoot | | OT Hours | | | |
M	LABOR	No.	Rate	Days	Rate	1.5	2.0	ESTIMATED	ACTUAL
234	Daniel								
235	Beth								
236	Owen								
237	Miss Wright								
238	Pierce								
239	Joe								
240	Dr. Jane								
241	Dr. Joseph								
242	Orderly 1								
243	Orderly 2								
244									

Appendix VI

M	TALENT LABOR	No.	Travel Rate	Shoot Days	Rate	OT Hours 1.5	OT Hours 2.0	ESTIMATED	ACTUAL
245									
246									
247									
248									
249									
250									
251									
252									
253									
254									
255									
256									
257									
258									
259									
260									
261									
262									
263									
264									
265									
						Sub-total M			
						PT/P&W			
266	Talent Agency Fees				20%				
267	Talent Payroll Service								
268	Talent Wardrobe Allowance								
269	Other								
270									
						TOTAL M			

N	TALENT EXPRESS	Amount	Rate	X	ESTIMATED	ACTUAL
271	Talent Air Fares					
272	Talent Hotels					
273	Talent Ground Transportation					
274	Other					
275	Other					
276						
				TOTAL N		

O	POST PRODUCTION LABOR	Amount	Rate	X	ESTIMATED	ACTUAL
277	Post Supervisor					
278	Off-line Editor					
279	Assistant Editor					
280						
281						
			Sub-total O			
			PT/P&W			
			TOTAL O			

P	POST PRODUCTION EXPENSES	Amount	Rate	X	ESTIMATED	ACTUAL
282	Film To Tape Transfer	8	250		2,000	2,389.75
283	Tape To Tape Transfer					
284	Telecine DVE					
285	Film Gate					
286	Transfer Stock					159.75
287						
288	Off-line Edit					
289	Off-line Digitize					
290	Off-line Media Storage					
291	Off-line Stock					
292						
293	Digital Graphics					
294	Digital Rotoscoping					
295	Digital Compositing					
296	Digital Stock					
297						
298	On-line Conform					
299	On-line DVE					
300	On-line Stock					
301	Character Generator					
302	Title Camera					
303	Edited Master					
304	Sub-masters					
305						
306	VO/ADR					
307	Music					
308	Sound Effects					1,800.00
309	Foley Studio					
310	Audio Laydown					
311	Audio Mix					
312	Audio Layback					
313	Audio Stock					
314	Playback & Master Audio					
315						
316	Dubs					
317	Standards Conversion					
318	Satellite Transmission					

Appendix VI

P	POST PRODUCTION EXPENSES	Amount	Rate	X	ESTIMATED	ACTUAL
319						
320	Stock Footage					
321	Animation					
322	Film Editing					
323	Opticals					
324	Negative Cutting					
325	IPs and Answer Prints					
326	Tape to Film Transfer					
327	Closed Captions					
328						
329						
				TOTAL P	2,000	4,349.50

"Daughter" 35mm Thesis Budget
2001

Running Time: 10 Minutes

Shooting Days: 9

Shooting Ratio: 10:1

New Stock?   Yes

Includes Variable Pricing

Meets MINIMUM Delivery Reqs.

Cutting Ratio: 3:1

Prepared By: N. Senger

Acct#	Category Title	Page	Total
1000	CAST/DAY PLAYERS/EXTRAS	1	$0
	Total Above-The-Line		**$0**
1500	FILM/SOUND STOCK	1	$2,384
2000	PRODUCTION LABORATORY/TRANSFER	1	$3,356
2500	EQUIPMENT RENTAL	1	$430
3000	PRODUCTION DESIGN	2	$1,863
3500	SET MANAGEMENT	2	$63
4000	OFFICE MANAGEMENT	2	$379
9999	OVER PRODUCTION BUDGET	2	$486
4500	CATERING AND CRAFT SERVICES	3	$1,821
	Total Production		**$10,782**
5000	EDITING EQUIPMENT/EXPENDABLES	3	$81
5500	POST LABORATORY/TRANSFER	3	$3,325
6000	NEGATIVE CUTTING	3	$2,239
6500	TITLES	4	$468
7000	VISUAL AND OPTICAL EFFECTS	4	$144
7500	MUSIC/SCORING	4	$13
8000	PUBLICITY/FESTIVAL	4	$171
8500	OTHER POST-PRODUCTION COSTS	4	$200
	Total Post-Production		**$6,641**
	10% Contingency		$1,742
	TOTAL ABOVE-THE-LINE		**$0**
	TOTAL BELOW-THE-LINE		**$17,423**
	TOTAL ABOVE & BELOW-THE-LINE		**$17,423**
	GRAND TOTAL		**$19,165**

Appendix VI

CHART OF ACCOUNTS

Acct#	Description	Acct#	Description
1000	**CAST/DAY PLAYERS/EXTRAS**	**4500**	**CATERING AND CRAFT SERVICES**
1001	CAST TRAVEL	4501	CATERING
1002	CAST PER DIEM	4502	CRAFT SERVICE
1500	**FILM/SOUND STOCK**	**5000**	**EDITING EQUIPMENT/EXPENDABLES**
1501	RAW FILM STOCK	5001	AVID
1502	RAW SOUND STOCK	5002	SOUND DESIGN
		5003	MIXING
2000	**PRODUCTION LABORATORY/TRANSFER**		
2001	NEGATIVE PROCESS/PREP	**5500**	**POST LABORATORY/TRANSFER**
2002	DAILIES VIDEO TRANSFER	5501	PRINTING
		5502	OPTICAL SOUND TRANSFER
2500	**EQUIPMENT RENTAL**	5503	FINAL RANK TRANSFER
2501	EQUIPMENT ROOM		
2502	GRIP TRUCK EXPENDABLES	**6000**	**NEGATIVE CUTTING**
2503	SOUND EXPENDABLES	6001	NEGATIVE CONFORMING
3000	**PRODUCTION DESIGN**	**6500**	**TITLES**
3001	SET DESIGN	6501	TITLES
3003	PROPS		
3004	WARDROBE	**7000**	**VISUAL AND OPTICAL EFFECTS**
3006	SPECIAL EFFECTS	7001	FADES/DISSOLVES
3099	ADDENDUM A		
		7500	**MUSIC/SCORING**
3500	**SET MANAGEMENT**	7501	SCORING
3501	CONTINUITY		
		8000	**PUBLICITY/FESTIVAL**
4000	**OFFICE MANAGEMENT**	8001	PRESS KITS
4001	SHIPPING	8002	VHS DUBBING
4002	TELEPHONE	8003	PRINTING
4003	OFFICE SUPPLIES	8004	MAILOUT/DISTRIBUTION
9999	**OVER PRODUCTION BUDGET**	**8500**	**OTHER POST-PRODUCTION COSTS**
9999	OVER PRODUCTION BUDGET	8501	POST-SHIPPING

"Daughter" 35mm Thesis Budget
2001

Running Time: 10 Minutes

Shooting Days: 9

Includes Variable Pricing

Meets MINIMUM Delivery Reqs.

Shooting Ratio: 10:1

New Stock? Yes

Cutting Ratio: 3:1

Prepared By: N. Senger

Acct#	Description	Amount	Units	X	Rate	Subtotal	Total
1000	**CAST/DAY PLAYERS/EXTRAS**						
1001	CAST TRAVEL						$0
1002	CAST PER DIEM						$0
						Total for 1000	**$0**
	Total Above-The-Line						**$0**
1500	**FILM/SOUND STOCK**						
1501	RAW FILM STOCK						
	Kodak Vision 35mm 320T (lo...	4,000	Feet		0.34	1,360	
	Kodak Vision 35mm 320T (sh...	2,500	Feet		0.19	475	
	Kodak Vision 35mm 500T (sh...	2,500	Feet		0.19	475	
	Kodak Vision 35mm 500T (en...	200	Feet		0.10	20	$2,330
1502	RAW SOUND STOCK						
	DAT Tape (125min)	9	Days		6.04	54	$54
						Total for 1500	**$2,384**
2000	**PRODUCTION LABOTATORY/TRANSFER**						
2001	NEGATIVE PROCESS/PREP						
	Process/Prep Charges	9,000	Feet		0.11	990	
	Cans/Handling		Allow		35	35	
	Test Process/Prep Charges	200	Feet		0.11	22	$1,047
2002	DALIES VIDEO TRANSFER						
	One Light AVID Transfer	9,000	Feet		0.25	2,250	
	Recon, BetaSP Stock (30min)	0	Days		9.00	0	
	Tests AVID Transfer	200	Feet		0.25	50	
	Beta SP Stock (30min) - Test	1	Tape		9.00	9	$2,309
						Total For 2000	**$3,356**
2500	**EQUIPMENT RENTAL**						
2501	EQUIPMENT ROOM						
	ER Use Fee	1	Flat		100	100	
	Camera Rental	1	Flat		176.40	176	$276
2502	GRIP TRUCK EXPENDABLES						
	Fuel		Allow	0	35	0	
	Truck Rental - Approved Over . . .		Allow		124.23	124	$124

Acct#	Description	Amount	Units	X	Rate	Subtotal	Total
2500	**EQUIPMENT RENTALS (cont.)**						
2503	SOUND EXPENDABLES						
	Batteries		Allow		30	30	$30
						Total for 2500	**$430**
3000	**PRODUCTION DESIGN**						
3001	SET DESIGN						
	Design Elements		Allow		600	600	$600
3003	PROPS						
	Properties (dolls)		Allow		300	300	$300
3004	WARDROBE						
	Miscellaneous		Allow		50	50	$50
3099	ADDENDUM A						
	Addendum A	1	Flat		863	863	$863
						Total for 3000	**$1,863**
3500	**SET MANAGEMENT**						
3501	CONTINUITY						
	Recon. BetaSP Stock (30min)	2	Tapes		9	18	
	Polaroid	9	Days		5	45	$63
						Total for 3500	**$63**
4000	**OFFICE MANAGEMENT**						
4001	SHIPPING						
	Production Shipping		Allow		300	300	$300
4002	TELEPHONE						
	Long Distance		Allow		48	48	$48
4003	OFFICE SUPPLIES						
	Postage	1	All		31	31	$31
						Total for 4000	**$379**
9999	**OVER PRODUCTION BUDGET**						
9999	OVER PRODUCTION BUDGET						
	OVER PRODUCTION BUDGET	1			486	486	$486
							$0
						Total For 9999	**$486**
4500	**CATERING AND CRAFT SERVICES**						
4501	CATERING						
	Provided Meals	9	Days	30	6	1,620	$1,620
4502	CRAFT SERVICE						
	Craft Service		Allow		201	201	$201
						Total for 4500	**$1,821**
	Total Production						**$10,782**

Acct#	Description	Amount	Units	X	Rate	Subtotal	Total
5000	**EDITING EQUIPMENT/EXPENDABLES**						
5001	AVID						
	Recon, BetaSP Stock (10 min)	2	Tapes	0	7	0	
	VHS Stock (10min)	1	Tapes		0.94	1	$1
5002	SOUND DESIGN						
	DA-88 Stock (60min)	10	Tapes		6.74	67	$67
5003	MIXING						
	Pre-dub/Final Mix DA-88 Stock	2	Tapes		6.74	13	$13
						Total For 5000	**$81**
5500	**POST LABORATORY/TRANSFER**						
5501	PRINTING						
	First Trial Print	900	Feet		1	900	
	Additional Trial Prints	900	Feet	2	0.50	900	
	Interpositive	900	Feet	0	1.28	0	
	Cans/Handling		Allow		35	35	
	Lo-Con	900	Feet	0	0.54	0	$1,835
5502	OPTICAL SOUND TRANSFER						
	Sound Sync	1	Flat		40	40	
	Sound Stock	1	Flat		200	200	
	Optical Sound Transfer	900	Feet		0.305	275	$515
5503	FINAL RANK TRANSFER						
	Supervised Color Timing	3	Hours		325	975	
	New BetaSP Stock (10min)	1	Tape	0	11.54	0	$975
						Total For 5500	**$3,325**
6000	**NEGATIVE CUTTING**						
6001	NEGATIVE CONFORMING						
	Conforming	240	Cuts		8.50	2,040	
	Setup	2	Reels		25	50	
	Extra Work (Drop-in of Titles)	2	Hours	0	30	0	
	Checkboarding Leader	990.0	Feet		0.15	149	$2,239
						Total For 6000	**$2,239**
6500	**TITLES**						
6501	TITLES						
	Photographic Charges	25	Cards		10	250	
	Kodaliths		Allow		50	50	
	Color Negative Film Stock	200	Feet		0.46	92	
	Processing	200	Feet		0.11	22	
	Work Print	200	Feet		0.27	54	$468
						Total For 6500	**$468**

Acct#	Description	Amount	Units	X	Rate	Subtotal	Total
7000	**VISUAL AND OPTICAL EFFECTS**						
7001	FADES/DISSOLVES						
	Fades	52	Fades		2	104	
	Disolves	10	Dissol...		4	40	$144
						Total For 7000	**$144**
7500	**MUSIC/SCORING**						
7501	SCORING						
	DA-88 Stock (60min)	2	Tape		6.74	13	$13
						Total For 7500	**$13**
8000	**PUBLICITY/FESTIVAL**						
8001	PRESS KITS						
	Press Kits	20	Kits		3	60	$60
8002	VHS DUBBING						
	News VHS Stock (10min)	41	Tapes		0.94	39	
	Labels		Allow		30	30	$69
8003	PRINTING						
	B&W Video Box Covers	20	Covers		0.25	5	
	B&W One Sheets	1	Posters		10	10	$15
8004	MAILOUT/DISTRIBUTION						
	VHS Library Rate	20	Tapes		1.35	27	
	Poster Tube Library Rate	0	Posters		2.35	0	$27
						Total For 8000	**$171**
8500	**OTHER POST-PRODUCTION COSTS**						
8501	POST-SHIPPING						
	Post-Shipping		Allow		200	200	$200
						Total For 8500	**$200**
	Total Post-Production						**$6,641**
	10% Contingency						**$1,742**
	TOTAL ABOVE-THE-LINE						**$0**
	TOTAL BELOW-THE-LINE						**$17,423**
	TOTAL ABOVE & BELOW-THE-LINE						**$17,423**
	GRAND TOTAL						**$19,165**

additional photography: Filming that occurs after principal photography has been completed. Additional photography is sometimes used for re-shoots.

ADR: Automatic dialogue replacement. *See* looping.

agent: A handler who represents above- or below-the-line talent. Their primary function is to secure work for their clients.

ancillary markets: One or more subsidiary markets for a work of authorship that is closely related to another market in the same work. For example, the right to make a movie available on pay-TV is probably ancillary to the right to make it available on commercial television.

animation: The photographing of a series of drawings or inanimate objects each showing a slight movement from the one before so they appear to be moving when they are projected back to an audience.

answer print: The first print in release form that will be checked before making additional release prints.

assistant director: The crew member responsible for delegating the director's instructions and making sure the cast and crew are in their required positions at the right time.

Avid: A name-brand Macintosh-based, nonlinear digital editing system.

cast: (**n**) The actors in a film. (**v**) To select actors to portray characters in a film.

casting director: Person responsible for selecting lead and supporting actors for a film.

CGI: Computer graphics imagery. The use of computer graphics to create or enhance special effects.

cinematographer: Person responsible for the camera and lighting design to achieve the director's vision and then capturing that vision on film.

composer: Person who writes the instrumental score for a film.

costume designer: Person responsible for creating costumes for film and television.

craft service: Crew members responsible for feeding the cast and crew in between meals on set.

crew: Below-the-line workers on a set.

development: The process of perfecting a film script so it is ready to shoot.

dialogue editor: A sound editor who edits the dialogue track.

director: The primary creative and artistic force behind a film. Person in charge of actors' performances on camera and determining the overall look and feel of the film.

director of photography: *See* cinematographer.

distribution: Process by which prints of a film are sent to theaters for exhibition.

documentary: A nonfiction film without actors.

dolly: Piece of equipment on which the camera is mounted in order to achieve smooth motion in any direction.

editor: Person responsible for creating a successful narrative by joining together the separate shots of film.

exhibition: A commercial presentation of a film for the public.

experimental: A film that is more visual and less narrative in nature.

extras: Background actors who do not have any lines of dialogue.

feature: A full-length motion picture.

film festival: A program of film exhibitions used to showcase new films. They often occur annually and last several days. Some of the more prominent festivals include the Cannes Film Festival, Sundance, and Slamdance.

film stock: The raw material used to record photographic images.

filmmaker: General term used to refer to the person who has significant control over a movie such as a director or producer.

Foley: Post-production process by which certain sounds within a motion picture are created by first watching the scene and then simulating effects to match the onscreen action.

FX editor: Sound editor who edits the special effects tracks.

gaffer: Person responsible for lighting a scene as directed by the cinematographer. Also known as the chief electrician.

genre: A category of film characterized by a particular style such as a comedy, drama, or Western.

high definition: The highest-quality digital video image available.

location manager: Person responsible for finding and attaining sites for shooting the film.

looping: Post-production process by which actors re-dub inaudible production dialogue.

mixing: Integrating all the various soundtracks of a film into one.

narrative: A story.

networking: Making contacts within the industry that will be beneficial to launching or helping a career in Hollywood.

opticals: Visual effects traditionally achieved with the help of an optical printer. These effects generally involve the combination of two or more images onto one piece of film, for example, freeze frames, fades, dissolves, or wipes.

physical effects: Mechanical effects such as explosions that take place on the set during the shoot.

picture lock: Term for the film once editing is complete and the sound is ready to be added.

post-production: The final phase of the filmmaking process. It includes everything after a film has finished shooting.

pre-dub: Cleaning, editing, and preparing of all soundtracks for the final mix.

pre-production: Everything that takes place before filming commences.

producer: Person who is ultimately responsible for the success or failure of a film and the person who generally oversees a project from initial concept to release.

production: General term to describe the actual filming of a movie or the movie being filmed.

production assistant: An entry level gofer position who works on a film set or in a production office.

production designer: Person responsible for the overall look of the picture as it pertains to form, color, and texture.

production manager: The person who supervises the budget, hires the crew, approves expenses, and ensures that all departments are doing their jobs efficiently.

production sound: Dialogue and some effects that are recorded during production.

prop master: Person who is responsible for the acquisition or manufacturing of props and for supervising all aspects of their use on set.

pulling focus: The process by which the assistant cameraman moves the lens during filming to adjust for movement between the camera and the subject without losing a sharp image.

reel: A visual résumé on video used by directors, cinematographers, and others that contains samples of their work.

re-recording mixer: The sound mixer responsible for mixing the dialogue, music, sound effects, and Foley.

runner: Production assistant whose primary duty is to run errands.

scene: A segment of the script using only one location, or a particular character, ending only in a change of location, time, or space.

score: A film's musical composition.

screenplay: A script intended for motion picture production.

screenwriter: Person who writes a screenplay.

screenwriting: Writing characters, dialogue, and situations specifically meant to be enacted on film.

script: *See* screenplay.

set: An area used for filming.

shot: The basic unit of film structure.

sound design: The audio component of a movie.

sound editor: General term for the person who edits the soundtrack.

sound effects: Sounds added during post-production that do not include dialogue, music, or narration.

spec script: A script written, but not commissioned, in order to sell to potential buyers.

Steadicam: A camera that is physically attached to a camera operator with a mechanical harness that eliminates an operator's motion.

studio: A company that produces, finances, and distributes films. The larger studios house sound stages and other filmmaking facilities.

stunt coordinator: Person responsible for making sure that stunts are safely choreographed and executed.

telecine: The process of transferring moving images from film to video, including frame rate and color correction.

visual effects: Effects created for the visual portion of a film in order to enhance an image, create something that wasn't originally there, or create an element that would be dangerous or otherwise impossible to film live.

FREDERICK LEVY is the author of several books about the entertainment industry. *The Hollywood Way* (St. Martin's Press, 2002) is an examination of the skills that make one successful in Hollywood; it then shows how to apply these same skills to find success in any career (www.thehollywoodway.com). *Hollywood 101: The Film Industry* (Renaissance, 2000), a two-time *Los Angeles Times* best-seller, is a survey of the film business in which Levy interviewed dozens of working industry professionals about getting started in a Hollywood career (www.hollywood-101.com). *The Ultimate Boy Band Book* (Pocket Books, 2000) is a young adult book about the boy band phenomenon in which Levy interviewed many of today's top teen music acts about the youth dominated music scene. *Short Films 101* is Levy's fourth book.

Aside from his writing chores, Levy is also the founder of Management 101. The firm guides the careers of actors, writers, and directors. Prior to forming a management firm, Levy was the associate producer of *Frailty* for Lions Gate Films, starring Bill Paxton and Matthew McConaughey.

For over eight years, Levy was the vice president of development and production at Marty Katz Productions. While there, the company produced *The Great Raid* for Miramax Films, directed by John Dahl, and starring Benjamin Bratt and James Franco; *The Four Feathers* for Miramax Films and Paramount Pictures, directed by Shekhar Kapur, and starring Wes Bentley and Heath Ledger; *Impostor* for Dimension films, directed by Gary Fleder, and starring Gary Sinise and Madeline Stowe; *Reindeer Games* for Dimension Films, directed by John Frankenheimer, and starring Ben Affleck and Charlize Theron; James Cameron's *Titanic* for Paramount Pictures and Twentieth Century Fox; *Mr. Wrong* for Touchstone Pictures, starring Ellen DeGeneres; and *Man of the House* for Walt Disney Pictures starring Chevy Chase and Jonathan Taylor Thomas. Before joining Marty Katz Productions, Frederick worked for InterMedia/Film Equities, Inc., which financed and packaged films.

Frederick began his Hollywood career as a studio guide at Universal Studios Hollywood. He got his start in television working as a guest coordinator on more than a dozen shows, including *Love Connection* and *Studs.* He also worked in professional radio as producer of *The Morning Magazine* on KWNK, Los Angeles, and the syndicated *Then and Now* and *The Celebrity DJ Party,* both of which he also created.

Levy graduated from the University of Southern California with a B.S. in business/marketing. He currently teaches film classes at UCLA Extension, the USC School of Cinema-Television, and the Los Angeles branch of Boston University. Consistently busy with a multitude of diverse media projects, Frederick is most proud of his work with the Starlight Foundation, for which he produced two celebrity charity benefits that raised money to help seriously ill children.

Levy is an avid speaker on the lecture circuit, having lectured at Harvard, Yale, NYU, USC, AFI, and Rutgers, and numerous writer and actor seminars throughout the country. He has been a featured guest on many TV and radio talk shows, including *Entertainment Tonight,* CNN, Fox News, MTV, VH1, and CBS News.